John G. Claxton

She of the Holy Light

John G. Claxton

She of the Holy Light

ISBN/EAN: 9783337248925

Printed in Europe, USA, Canada, Australia, Japan

Cover: Foto ©Lupo / pixelio.de

More available books at **www.hansebooks.com**

SHE OF THE HOLY LIGHT

BY

JOHN G. CLAXTON.

WESTERN AUTHORS' PUBLISHING ASSOCIATION.

NEW YORK:
WORLD BUILDING

SAN FRANCISCO:
DONOHOE BUILDING.

1893

Entered according to the Act of Congress, in the year 1893, by
THE AUTHOR,
In the office of the Librarian of Congress, at Washington, D. C.

קוּמִי אוֹרִי כִּי־בָא אוֹרֵךְ
וּכְבוֹד יְהוָה עָלַיִךְ זָרָח

Isaiah LX, 1.

CHAPTER FIRST.

> "As whirlwinds in the south pass through; so it cometh from the desert, from a terrible land."
> "For thus hath the Lord said unto me, 'Go set a watchman, let him declare what he seeth'."
>
> Isaiah xxi. 1-6

HELL WAS MOVED!..............The cattle stood still beneath a burning sun. Herds were crowded together panting and breathless. The earth throbbed with an electric thrill. A tremor crept through the herds. Lightning flashed. The cattle started, lifted their heads, sniffed the air, bellowed, reared and plunged—then swept on, wildly, madly; the dust, darkness, and lightning intermingling like the sulphurous flames of the nethermost depths. The powers of evil united, changing the cattle to monsters that left desolation behind them...... They might have been drawing the chariot of the Apocalypse.

Amidst all this, a child's voice cried out: "Mamma!" in appealing, frightened tones.

No answer came to the helpless cry. The strange sounds grew more appalling. Into the semi-darkness an Indian leaped beside the child, bent his ear to the ground, and sprang up. Then touching the child, he said: "Be not afraid. Garangula will save thee!"

A struggle began, mighty, swift, terrible—between one man and a thousand affrighted beasts.

Oh, the horror of that mad stampede! The helpless, hopeless wrangle of hoofs and horns; the plunging, leaping, struggling with all the fury of demons!

The Indian laid the child down, bared his breast to the foe, and sweeping his arm in a circle, cried out: "O Great Spirit!"

The thunders rolled and muttered and crashed.

Garangula, the Indian, stood still. The lightning sent forth flames in hellish glee. Then with the abandon of a god, he flung himself on the ground in front of the child....a great bull, his eyes of fire, stilled like an arrested demon, poised for an instant, and the furious hosts divided and swept on.

By Garangula's side was a woman, whose form radiated a strange light.

"Great Spirit! Great Light!" he cried.

CHAPTER SECOND.

> "............................ The elements
> So mixed in him, that Nature might stand up,
> And say to all the world,
> This was a man."
>
> Shakespeare.

THE sun had set. A crescent moon hung in the sky. Stray clouds passed each other bringing messages from an unknown world. Cattle rested in sphinx-like repose, their great, pathetic eyes turned to the hills beyond. Over all appeared a green, suggestive of an initiation into some mystic Order. One could not look on the scene without deep reverence and a closer sympathy with all things.

Near a streamlet, in the Techauana Valley of Texas, twelve or fifteen cowboys flung themselves on the ground.

Far away, on a gently sloping hill, stood a man whose dark face, deepened by the shadows, seemed an antique bronze against the sunset sky. In his repose, was blended the strength of the Anglo-Saxon with the grace of the Oriental. Raising his arm slowly toward the hills, he said: "O hills of beauty! Garangula's fathers called ye Chihuahua! Ah, the Great Spirit lingered here then. Where are Garangula's people? Have they journeyed to the Happy Hunting-Grounds? Garangula looks up at the great lights in the night-time and thinks of the Happy Hunting-Grounds. Sometimes he hears a voice, and again he sees a light among these hills and rocks. And the Great Spirit comes near and touches him.

"Garangula has heard that it is written in the white man's book: 'In the unknown past, when the wily Indian Chieftain led hither in peace or in conquest, the untamed hearts of his tribe to enjoy the worship of the Great Spirit, what a thrill of delight must have filled the warrior's breast when he first saw these hills! The inspiration must have been divine, though in a savage breast, that made the red man name these hills Tehuacana.'

"'Though in a savage breast!' How differs the white man from the savage? And yet, as Garangula looks over at the white man's home, it seems strange—and something cries out for that which is lost."

An expression, like the light rising in the east on a gray day, o'erspread Garangula's face. He walked on. The light grew brighter, the mystic green vibrated nearer. He felt enveloped in some mysterious power....

A strange sight met his gaze. Round a camp-fire, beside his own wigwams, wondrous forms moved with the same rhythm he had seen in the waving boughs; in the birds as they flew through the air, and in the waves as his canoe floated down the stream. He had so lived in all this beauty and poetry of motion, he was not surprised at what he saw; neither was he surprised at their wonderfully developed forms—he had seen only Indian women. These graceful women moved in softly flowing robes.

With a slow, rhythmic motion, floating dreamily, the curves and spirals blended, telling strange stories, interweaving dim legends with a dashing touch of their own times. In the soft twilight they clasped hands and danced in a circle—gently they sank in repose.

The Indian looked on with joy that was holy. He seemed not to breathe. A dark figure moved from out the shadows. She held a child in her arms and bent over the camp-fire, singing in a weird tone, as she stirred the smouldering embers. The light flared. With a sudden inspiration, one of the group sprang up and enacted a scene. Astarte and Dionysius, Ariadne and Bacchus, and all the gods of lust sanctioned her rites. Shades of darkness! It was the Dance of Death. Garangula's face expressed no dismay; his breathing was slow and deep.

"Her spirit has of the strange color in the rainbow after the storm," he said.

The black figure still stirred the fire, and the light flared with a dying brilliancy. The woman mingled with the reflection and seemed a living flame—one more spiral motion downward and she disappeared in a shadowy cave. The camp-fire sank into darkness, the singing ceased.

From out the darkness arose the woman with the Light about her. The Indian's face was illumined. He bowed his head and said softly:

"The Lamp of the Great Spirit is beneath her feet.

"O Great Spirit! O Holy Light!"

CHAPTER THIRD.

"Thy shepherd's slumber, O king of Assyria; thy nobles shall dwell in the dust; thy people is scattered upon the mountains, and no man gathereth them."
Nahum iii. 18.

THE woman whose spirit partook of the strange color in the rainbow, looked at Her of the Light, then at the Indian. She knew they had rescued her child—through what power she did not understand. Awed by the appearance of the glorified form, the woman addressed herself to Garangula:

"You saved my child—I know not what to say."

"Then say nothing, O beautiful pale-face," he replied. "Let thy beauty speak. Then it becomes as the silence of the stars, the skies, the plains. Silence knows and speaks all things. Garangula hears it."

"How could you hear silence?" asked a little girl, springing from the bough of a tree.

"Garangula listens," he answered simply.

The woman was at a loss for words. Who was this strange man, in dress a savage, yet in speech a poet? She, who had moved among kings, felt humbled in the presence of his simplicity.

Jakusa, the little girl, who had been taking in every detail, could not restrain her curiosity any longer.

"Are you a real, live Indian? You don't look quite like one; tell us about yourself—an Indian story—I am dying to hear a story—anything, so it is real Indian."

They gathered around the camp-fire. The moonlight fell on the wigwams, making a background for a scene that was beautiful, poetic, strange.

Garangula sat by the door. His robe fell in folds on the ground, leaving his body bare to the waist. On his breast, joined with massive ornaments, hung a row of beads, curiously wrought. His hair was braided and looped with fox-tails, in his ears were heavy rings, and he wore a turban that contrasted strangely with his other apparel.

"There is little to tell," he began. "Garangula, the Indian, is a cowboy, tending the cattle by day, and sleeping on the ground at night. He cares for herds owned by an English lord, learning much from him. He loves to listen to him read, telling of the countries beyond the seas. The world is large, as he has dreamed.

"Garangula's mother belonged to the race of the red man, and was stolen from her tribe by the white man. Among them was one who had come from a far-off country. He loved her for her beauty. He was kind to her, but she begged to follow her people to this place. The wigwam on the side of the hill yonder, was her home. They have gone on a journey—the dwelling-place is empty. These hills were left Garangula by his father. He will keep this spot wild and free forever, so those who have gone on a journey to the Happy Hunting-Grounds will come back, and not feel strange. Garangula is glad the pale-faces have journeyed hither and tarried on his ground. It may be his people will return now."

He was silent a moment, then said: "Garangula was happy in the wigwam on the side of the hill, listening to the stories his mother told him. How the white man had driven her kindred toward the setting sun till they reached this spot. It was once an Indian village. Over these hills the Indians roamed as the deer, the antelope and buffalo. Soon pale-faces began peering about, and the white man stole along the deep ravines after dark, and measured the land.

"The war-dance is no longer seen, and the echoes of the war-whoop have long since died out in the valleys."

Garangula rose, and looking across the hills and valleys, said, "O, white man, do you not feel strange? You are in the dwelling-place of another. The footprints of those whose faces have turned toward the west, cry out against you, 'Where shall the Indian rest?' Their wigwams are gone, their arms are scattered and broken—

they have left you no title to these hills but blood."

A movement from Jakusa recalled him, and he resumed his story.

"An old man going on a journey, bade Garangula come to him. These were the words he spoke: 'Garangula, listen! On a day like this, I witnessed the farewell of an Indian Chief, to the hills the red man loved. That grim and massive warrior was thy grandfather. He stood on Rocky Bluff—the last of his unnumbered tribe, his form erect, his arms folded, and head thrown back. Thus in the glory of his savage life, alone, unattended, he stood on the brow of the hill near thy home, and surveyed the scene. Then, with one last farewell look, the Chieftain turned, and with bowed head, bent his course toward the setting sun.'"

Garangula was silent. His head sank on his breast, then he walked down the valley whence his ancestor had departed.

CHAPTER FOURTH.

"And I will make them and the places round about my hill a Blessing."
Ezekiel xxxiv. Verse 4.

THE sunlight fell on the grand old hills that no longer echoed the Indian war-whoop.

In the door of a wigwam, stood the woman whose child was rescued. A number of girls had gathered around her, listening. She told them a wonderful story of beauty and freedom. A weird look came from eyes that flashed a green color in their intensity, giving the feeling that this unknown woman knew more than she revealed. A Greek nose with the mouth of a Cleopatra, displaying characteristics so complex, one was at a loss to know what race claimed her.

She was born in Cuba, it was said, and yet a

stranger influence of the stars took her mother, early in life, to New Orleans, where the daughter's character was unfolded in the midst of the brilliant French society that flourished in the Crescent City of those days. It was not many years before she declared her freedom from its conventionalities, pursuing life in her own way, which was at variance with that of people adhering strictly to every point of the Decalogue. It was whispered that she was a princess, whose ancestry dated to a more remote period than any crown of the present century. This, and her brilliant beauty gave her access to nearly every court of Europe. But she returned with increasing affection to her native home. "The emotions and passions that burn in my soul like the fires of hell, are in harmony with this tropical country," she would say. "One could be great here—if it were worth the while.

"I should dare to pluck yonder star, if I wished it. Had I lived in those olden days, I should have reveled in being a part of an emperor's conquest, dragged through the streets of Rome. How the world would applaud were my voice heard in song! But no one shall know. The Master will keep my secret. And ———some day."

Was she a prophetess, a great teacher, or tempter? She breathed and moved as a savage or a goddess, the colors of her robe blending and vibrating till one was intoxicated. The light, wonderful hair, with its tone of green here and there, was wound around the head and bound with a fillet of gold. To-day she seems living music—a breathing poem, as she speaks to her disciples.

Beyond, at the foot of the hill, stood She of the Holy Light. The drapery about her head touched the softly flowing mantle of gray, the color seen in the sky before the sun bursts forth.

She was looking at a cave whose beauty had been left undisturbed through all the ages. The Indian had slumbered peacefully on its rock bed and risen with the morning sun to continue his journey, leaving behind him no regrets, no longings. A spring gushed from the rock and flowed on in the stillness. Wild flowers grew in a tangle round the mouth of the cave. There, in the softly swaying grass, with the butterflies lighting on her sunny head, lay a child, smiling. Beside her, was an Indian hatchet and bits of strange looking earthenware.

The motion of the grass grew swifter, the head of a snake raised itself—its eyes glistened in the sun as they became fixed for a moment on the woman, then glided toward the child. Soon it coiled itself around the arm of the child, who playfully touched the spots of bright color, and said, "Bootiful, bootiful," then stroked it caressingly. After a time, the lids drooped. The snake's eyes looked out with the expression that has so mystic a meaning, and the two slept.

She of the Holy Light said, "O Type of Innocence and Symbol of Wisdom, sleep on................. The secret of all harmony is Love."

CHAPTER FIFTH.

> "But be ye glad and rejoice forever in that which I create."
> Isaiah lxv. 18.

On the spot, where the night before the cowboys had camped, stood a tall, fair girl. Her white robe, caught up at the waist by a girdle, fell in graceful lines to her sandalled feet. The glory of morning was about her. She held in her hand a curious water-vessel found in the cave. She knelt and dipped water from the spring, and placing the vessel on her shoulder, her beautiful, white arm reaching up to the quaintly-carved handle, she climbed a steep, rocky place, and stood watching the purple sea in the east.

Taking the jug from her shoulder she leaned

forward, holding her robe with one hand, and said:

"'Day unto day uttereth speech, and night unto night showeth knowledge.' Why cannot I find knowledge here? Is it because my soul is not in unison with these? What are these? What is harmony? We are told the highest expression of art would be the highest expression of life. What is Art? What is Beauty? Are Beauty and Truth one? What is the relation between nature and truth? Does the highest expression of Life, Beauty, Art, lead to the same end?"

Descending the cliff, she seated herself upon a rock, took a paper from her bosom, and drew curious figures.

Then she tore the paper into bits and dropped them on the ground, speaking aloud: "'I am more and more plunged into chaos. The more light I receive, the darker it grows.' Will this beautiful art I am studying, help my soul to rise? Will it lead to that harmony of being for which I long all the days. A wise man hath said: 'The soul which stops to contemplate its wings will never rise.'"

She bowed her head, her lips moved in prayer. She arose, and slowly wandered on. The rays of the rising sun were playing on the sleepers, who still dreamed in the wigwams on Tehuacana Hills. Soon Jakusa bounded out, followed by Dixie, a big, black dog. Seeing the girl with the water-vessel on her shoulders, Jakusa cried:

"Rachel, Rachel, you were a long while at the spring. But you must be tired. Give me the jug, I'll take it to Aunt Dinah. See, she is standing there shading her eyes with her hand and looking for you."

"How picturesque she looks in the tent door," said Rachel, "the sun shining full on her dark face, bringing out her brilliant attire!"

Jakusa returned; then she and Rachel gathered wild flowers. When they entered the wigwams, they placed each one's favorite flower beside the couch.

"These," whispered Jakusa, with a caressing touch, "are for Zulona, whom Garangula called 'the beautiful pale-face.' I wonder why you always put white flowers by Wanda!"

"I wonder myself," replied Rachel, as she knelt and kissed the little sleeper. Zulona was its mother, but "Our Baby" she was called, and a stranger could not have told to whom she belonged.

An interesting group they made, Rachel kneeling over the baby who lay in an attitude of exquisite repose. One little hand was held out as though giving. Rachel put the flowers in the hand, and smiled as she thought, "The attitude of giving and receiving is the same. The meaning may be deeper than we know."

Soon a deep, authoritative voice rang out, "Is you chillun 'bout ready for breakfas'? You know ole Dinah don't like to wait."

Aunt Dinah ruled the domestic life of the camp. She prepared their simple food as no one can but those of her race.

"Everything has so much 'expression' about it," said Jakusa, as she looked slyly at Aunt Dinah.

"Spression! spression! Ole Dinah don't heah

nothin' else but dat nowadays," she replied, walking away with great dignity.

The sun was high in the heavens when Zulona, speaking to her followers, said, "Come."

They were soon standing on Rocky Bluff, the wild, picturesque scenery around them. Near by, was the wigwam that had been the romantic home of the dusky maiden, whose dark beauty had won the white man from the far-off country. Boughs o'ershadowed, vines crept about it, and grass grew round the door. It lay still and peaceful in the shadows, a relic of another age. One could almost fancy the Indian woman standing in the doorway, looking out with longing eyes across the hills and valleys. Was she happy in her captivity? Then came the picture of her with a papoose in her arms, the strange eyes looking at her questioningly. They sat under the trees, the long shadows about them; the child listened in awe as she told stories of the pale-faces. But the trees, the softly-waving boughs, to which they both talked and listened, told no stories. All was silence.

By-and-by the tones of a low, sweet voice were heard. Zulona said:

"The pictures have been painted for us, but we must see them through our own eyes."

She drew illustrations from the sky, the rocks, the trees and flowers. She gave a beautiful version of the wedding ring, showing the symbolical meaning of color from the lightest shades to the most complex combinations. Love was portrayed with the deep passion of Color. She sang the seven notes of music — the birds listened. A triumphant gleam flashed from her eyes. She showed the relation of the seven notes to the seven colors of the rainbow. Tones floated on the air and mingled with the colors till fancy played one false, and he saw the rainbow hung above him — each hue singing. She spoke of Beauty, declaring Ugliness to be a crime.

These were the last words Zulona spoke on Tehuacana Hills.

In the shadow of a great rock She of the Holy Light said: "Ah, they do not understand. I cannot reveal to them............The time is not yet."

CHAPTER SIXTH.

> "On hill-tops sown a little corn
> Like Lebanon with fruit shall bend;
> New life the city shall adorn;
> She shall like grass grow and extend."
> Psalm 72-9.

IT was high noon. Garangula walked toward the wigwams on the hills. The memory of that evening was as a vision.... He drew near the spot.... no gentle voices, no motion of the birds and waves greeted him. It had been a vision then. He looked long and earnestly—he moved towards the door by which he had sat. A paper was fastened near; there was writing on it. Ah, he could spell its meaning, thanks to the English lord. It was with difficulty, however, that he mastered the words:

"May those who have gone on a journey to

the Happy Hunting-Grounds, come to the dwelling-place of Garangula, the Indian, and not feel strange."

He folded the paper, put it in his bosom, and entered the wigwam. All was still. The valleys slept. The great plains stretched away in silence..... The shadows on the hills grew dim, the cattle began to low, the songs of birds became fainter and fainter, the snake uncoiled itself and slipped away in the dark shadows of the cave. But still the Indian moved not. He sat on the ground, his head bent forward, his eyes trying to pierce through all earthly vision. ....The moon hung full and round in the heavens. The Indian stepped forth.

"O Great Spirit," he said, his face turned upward, "O Great Spirit, guide Garangula, the Indian. O, ye hills and valleys and plains, Farewell!"

CHAPTER SEVENTH.

*"Hast thou entered into the spring of the sea? or
hast thou walked in the search of the depth?"*
Job 38:16.

THE tears over parting from those who have become dear to us, the joys at beholding them again; the very griefs and tragedies of this world prove that humanity is good the world over, and that its heart-strings throb in sympathy always. The departure or return of a steamer, bringing to mind the uncertainty of life on the billows, recalls this with great force. Those who have no personal interest give a blessing as the vessel leaves, a welcome when she returns.

On a May morning, when the steamer, "Martha Washington," moved slowly from the New York harbor, there was a group on board who did not correspond to the usual stereotyped list of passengers. On the forward deck, stood Zulona in a green-bronze costume, the green silk hood drawn far over her brow that had a shade of sadness on it as she looked back at the shore, and wondered what the future held for her. Close by, stood a woman, whose robe reminded one of the dove's breast and the olive leaf. Some old market women looked at her, and said: "It is a good omen; she will bring luck to the ship."

Jakusa, in a blue sailor costume, was investigating the ship and already making the acquaintance of the deck hands, Dixie by her side equally interested. Aunt Dinah sat on a camp-stool, her red kerchief tied on her head with the artistic effect of negro simplicity. At the further end of the deck was Rachel in a white flannel dress; she held Wanda in her arms, a thick, white shawl wound around her and the child, her face looking far out at sea. As the ship glided away in the distance, the folds of the white shawl seemed clouds. She looked a Madonna 'twixt sea and sky.

The "Martha Washington" was far out at

sea. The group that attracted so much attention when sailing, were sitting in silence. Zulona moved her arm toward the sea, and spoke aloud:

"Grand old sea, your power to grasp and slay, and with next morning's sun to move majestically over the ruin you have wrought, fills me with a wild, intoxicating delight. I envy you!"

A voice softly whispered: "'And there shall be no more sea.'"

At last, Zulona's mood changed. She said: "Rachel, look at the waves and you will learn a great lesson. Close your eyes and feel their influence. Do you recognize the difference between this and the waving boughs of the trees? How subtle that influence is! All rhythmic motion is salutary. There is a rhythm that excites one like martial music. I felt this keenly when in the Zoölogical Gardens, I saw a Bengal tiger striding up and down his cage—I had the same emotions when Salvini came on the stage, before the murder of Desdemona. And so we might continue, from the tranquil murmur of the meadow brook to the cyclone that sweeps the forest—from the light clouds on a summer day to the motion of the heavenly spheres."

"I don't understand, if the waves are so 'rhythmic' as you say, why they should make me so awful sick," said Jakusa.

Not waiting for an answer, she glanced at the woman of the Holy Light.

"Will you tell me?"

"My child, it is because you are not in harmony. You have a force within you that can overcome all things."

Jakusa's face brightened, and she went skipping down the deck singing:

> "'Love your neighbor as yourself,
> As the world you go traveling thro';
> Never sit down and frown,
> But paddle your own canoe.'"——

She whirled, came dancing back, and stopping in front of Aunt Dinah, began telling stories. When she had finished, she balanced on one toe and shocked Aunt Dinah with a glimpse of ballet life.

"Bress my soul! Whar did you learn dat? On 'de Bowery'? 'Pears to me dat's whar you larned 'most eberthing you know — must be a awful place; you ought to be thankful to de good Lawd you is fell in good han's. Whar did you say she foun' you?"

"In the slums, Aunt Dinah. You don't know where that is, but she found me there, in rags, crying for bread, for I was so hungry. The angel took me with her. Do you remember the day we reached the wigwams?"

"Yes, Law'—forgit dat day? Neber! Dat look on her face skeered ole Dinah so she dropped de ash-cake, jes' as she had it ready to eat."

Jakusa laughed,—"She frightened me once."

"She ought to skeer you ofner dan she do."

"Oh, Aunt Dinah, you don't know how much I'm improved—why they wouldn't know me on the Bowery now."

"Good thing fur you. I wonder she don't shake the life outin you sumtime."

"She just looks at me," smiled Jakusa. Then going nearer, she whispered: "Did I ever tell you about the time when I had a swearing fit on me, and how she looked at me?"

"No," said Aunt Dinah, in awed tones, "tell me."

"Well, one day I was so tired of being good, tired of seeing everyone else good, I felt I must do something. I went by myself and began to swear, imagining my companion who talked to me. I swore for both of us. I said everything I had ever heard, and then drew on my imagination, which is bigger in that line than some people's bank accounts. How I enjoyed it! More than anything I had known since my first square meal. All at once, in the middle of my most heavy part, as the stage players say, my tongue suddenly stopped—it wouldn't move—I tried it until I began to choke, but no use. Then a strange feeling came over me, I grew frightened and started to run, but stopped, for there the angel stood, with a Light in her face, I can't tell you what it looked like, but it made me fall on my knees and begin to say, 'Now I lay me'—"

"Den did she shake you? She ought to. ef she didn't."

"No, she just looked at me."

The two were silent a moment, then Jakusa continued: "Do you know, Aunt Dinah, I get awfully tired of civilized life, they call it?"

She was sitting on a steamer-chair, her head bent over her knee, looking a comical picture of dejection. "But I don't get tired so much now as I did at first."

"Humph!" and Aunt Dinah's nose went up in the air as she tied the handkerchief on her head a little tighter. The two were alone on deck, the others having gone to dinner—they had dined at the children's hour, much to Jakusa's disgust.

"You 'peared ter enjoy yoursef mighty at the wigwums," said Aunt Dinah.

"That wasn't like civilized life; it was better. I don't know what it was, but I liked it. And the Indian was grand, wasn't he? He made me think of a man I saw once in a place where my father took me — it's a real nice story, Aunt Dinah; let me tell it to you," and Jakusa brightened at the thought of a new conquest.

"You're gwine to tell me de truf now, chile?"

"I declare," and Jakusa held up her hand.

"When you does dat, I know it's so—you is a honest chile when you declar' fo' de Lawd. But la', how you do fool ole Dinah sumtimes, tellin' your great, long stories, er puttin' in eberything and me so enjoyin' it, and when jes' at de end you clap yo' han's an' say you made it up ebery bit. You'se a smart chile, Jak."

"And your ghost stories, Aunt Dinah, are they all true?" asked Jakusa, smiling.

"Ebery one uv 'em, I declar' fo' goodness," she replied, shaking her head solemnly and moving her body to and fro. "I neber see a chile, Jak, as could 'member like you; 'pears to me like you neber forgits anyt'ing, an' how glib you does say off dem lessons!"

"That's because I hate 'em so; I study just as hard as I can that I may get through."

"Oh, dat's it, am it? But go long wid yo' story."

"Well, my father took me to a place once, where they drink and play cards and swear. Oh, it was awful, but I liked it. People stirred and moved and I could breathe there." Then she portrayed the scenes as only a child can, growing more and more eloquent as the wide eyes and mouth of her auditor encouraged her.

When ready for the climax, Jakusa rose and

acted the scene, not without effect — hers was a receptive nature that had spent its tenderest years among tragic scenes, and she had learned much of expression at the wigwams.

"In the midst of all this," she said, "a woman screamed—such a scream! I can hear it now. At the door a big, burly man was dragging her by her long, jet-black hair. She was as white as the ghost you tell about, Aunt Dinah; her very lips were white, and her large, black eyes were the most beautiful I ever saw. The brute dragged her with her face turned upwards. I was awfully frightened, and a rough-looking, but kind man, took me up in his arms. I looked down on her face; it was so pale. It was all done so quickly and yet I remember everything. When she screamed a splendid-looking young fellow, who was playing cards, sprang up and rushed to her.

"'By what right do you interfere?' the ruffian cried.

"'By the eternal right of manhood,' the young man answered, and his voice rang out like a bell. A pistol flashed—in a second I was on the floor,

and the man who held me, struck the pistol up.
The ball whizzed over the young man's head and
lodged in the ceiling. It was an awful time, but
the woman was saved. Wasn't he brave to stand
there and defy that brute, when he knew he
was in danger of his life? Oh, I think it was
grand," and Jakusa bounded away quite satisfied with the effect of her recital on Aunt Dinah
and two or three sailors, who had stopped to
listen.

"I wonder fo' de Lawd ef dat chile been tellin'
me mo' lies! Jak," she called, "come back and
talk sum mo'. I ain't had no time to ax you
questions befo'. How ole is you, Jak?"

"Don't know—think I am about thirteen—
they didn't celebrate birthdays much where I
was a 'cub'."

"You'se been about lots fur a gal of yo' age,
hain't you?"

Jakusa, forgetting they were on the sea, said,
with an imitative air of wisdom: "Oh, a bit—
I've been from one end of this continent to the
other. My parents used to drag me from place to
place—at least, my father did, and my poor

mother had to go. She had to sing in the streets, and such singing, Aunt Dinah, I never heard. And ever since the Angel found me, we have been traveling. We went way to California, through Mexico, in the South, and at last stopped at the wigwams longer than anywhere. And, Aunt Dinah," she moved closer and spoke in a lower tone, "we did go to some of the most out-of-the-way places, and went in the strangest way. Sometimes in the night she'd wake me up and say, 'We must go,' and we would start out in the darkness. She always got to places where somebody was sick or starving to death. Sometimes we went to fine houses and everything would be grand, but it was always the same. I began to think everybody in the world was sorry about something, till we reached the wigwams, where all seemed different. Sometimes we stayed many weeks at the great places, and I was happier when we got to poor people, they seemed more contented. The Angel was always the same, and everybody looked at her sort of scared."

"Don't blame 'um," said Aunt Dinah; "she's enuf to skeer enybody."

"You ought to get her to tell you a story, Aunt Dinah."

"'Feard to—I bet she's seen ghosts."

CHAPTER EIGHTH.

"They shall lift up their voice, they shall sing for the majesty of the Lord, they shall cry aloud from the sea."
Isaiah 24=14.

It was night. All was quiet aboard the ship, "Martha Washington," and but for the waves washing on her sides, no sound was heard. Venus was rising, throwing a path of light over the sea. The voices of the stars spoke of strange and sudden dangers. Their echoes were heard in illimitable space, and the Silence answered, "My power is greater than all. The rest is in me."

She of the Holy Light stood alone upon the deck, the stillness of that fated night about her. The heavens were cloudless, the sea was calm, danger seemed far away. She looked toward the east. Who can describe her? No one can say aught but this, her face wore the look of Eternal Power and Eternal Youth.

The waning moon cast a pale light upon the waves as the ship went on her way. The passengers slumbered and dreamed of meeting friends on the morrow, for the journey was well-nigh ended.

From the stars the voices spake again, and the Silence answered, "I am Eternal!" A shadow passed over the face of the moon—the stars disappeared, one by one, as dark clouds rose on the horizon. Gradually the approaching dawn darkened, fog stole over the heavens and the sea. Soon a fog bell is heard. There is movement on deck. The fog thickens—the sky and sea grow darker. The dread sound is heard again and again. The captain's voice is hoarse and indistinct as he cries out his orders—the pilot stands on the bridge....She of the Holy Light is unobserved. She speaks aloud—her voice sounds like the whisperings of peace:

"O Thou Who rulest the stars! Thou Who art All in all! I call to Thee!"

The fog spreads over the ship like a pall. The waves grow higher, the ship sways, moves slower—ceases.... and the pilot hears a sound more ominous than the bells. Clearing the fog and the blackness, a huge object becomes visible; the pilot sees it and shivers. It is a ship! The resting vessel is powerless—nearer, nearer.

Oh, God! Can nothing avert the doom!

A great cry goes up in the night.

The ships heave and roll and cling like monsters of the deep, struggling for life. The unknown vessel gives one strong shiver, her masts are still a moment, then fall to the sea. Confusion reigns. Piercing cries of women and children rise above the frenzied curses of men, as they rush frantically in and out of the darkness—the yellow lights falling on horror, despair, resignation.

Heaven! Is there no help?

"The time has come," said She. A Light so radiant envelops her, the terror-stricken people pause. She stands there a living Invocation 'twixt man and God.

Lo! the Light o'erspreads the scene. The

people stand in awe. The Light grows more and more radiant about them............

All is silence.......The boats glide to and fro...... The perishing people rescued, the ill-fated ship careens lower and lower on its side, and disappears.

The Light intensified into a blaze of Glory ....then vanished.

CHAPTER NINTH.

> "We, ignorant of ourselves,
> Beg often our own harms, which the wise powers
> Deny us for our good; so find we profit
> By losing our prayers."
> — Shakespeare.

THE Master stood among his disciples. He said: "Art is the soul revealing itself.... It is a mystic Incarnation."

No one noticed a tall woman, closely veiled, enter the room and seat herself in the shadow. Many hours the Master continued talking of the Revelation.

At last, one by one, the pupils reluctantly departed. He turned to leave the room.

The woman rose and drew aside the heavy veil—"Zulona!" he cried.

"No, not the Zulona thou didst know, Master," she whispered, brokenly. "Her voice is gone. She is no longer Zulona."

"Great God! What hast thou done?" He looked at her keenly—this man who read men's souls.

"Thou hast committed a crime!" he said. "Why come to me? I am not a priest."

"Aye, thou art a high priest, O Master, and I come to thee. Wearily have I worked my way— in poverty and disguise. Restore my voice."

"Go, purge thy soul first," he answered. Then tenderly, as a father, he laid one hand on her head, while the other touched the white cross on his breast. "Child, confess."

A shiver ran through her frame.

"I will not," she answered.

He frowned. A moment, and his face softened.

"I will lead thee back to thy former soul-life; thou wilt yet know the truth within thine own soul."

"Not yet, not yet," she whispered.

"Thou, my first great pupil," he said mournfully, "Thou, who couldst sing as mortal ne'er sang before. Glad am I— yes, I rejoice that I took thee no further."

"I know much, my Master."

"Yea, yea," he replied, "but thou didst not enter the Holy of Holies."

Her head drooped low on her breast. At last she looked up defiantly and said: "I will restore my own voice. I will yet move the world. Until then, I will give the knowledge I have of thy teachings. When not moved, I can still speak in sweet tones; aye, not long ago, among the hills, I sang the seven notes." There flashed the same triumphant look seen when on Tehuacana Hills.

"Farewell." The veil was drawn, and with a panther-like movement she passed from the room.

The Master sighed.

Softly, like the sounds of Æolian harps, a voice spoke to him—the room was full of light. The Master listened, his eyes burning.

"Be not discouraged," said the voice. "The veiled woman goes forth, continuing her strange journey in life. She will at last faithfully represent thy doctrine. Thou shalt yet be glorious among those who love Art as that akin to the divine."

The voice ceased. The sunlight fell through the half-open door, and touched the cross on his breast. The great Master was alone.

CHAPTER TENTH.

> "A man's gift maketh room for him, and bringeth him before great men."
> Proverbs 18-16.

IN the suburbs of one of the capitals of the old world, stood a palace; though partly in ruins, its main features had been preserved for more than five centuries. A high wall of solid masonry enclosed grounds of many acres. Its massive gates of iron were opened but once in seven days; all who entered, must tarry until that time elapsed. This, with the past history of the palace and the peculiarities of the present owner, made it one of singular interest. Mazaro, the owner, could boast a long line of noble ancestors who had spent their lives in seclusion. This, no doubt, unfolded in him the wish to see and know all humanity, and his whole life was devoted to the study of what he called human nature. Sympathetic he was not, but possessed with an inordinate desire of knowing, merely for the power that knowledge brings. Those less informed, spoke of him as a mystic. It was said that they who tarried in the Strange Palace, left with a new and greater power. The gates were opened to the world, and perhaps no place ever entertained such dissimilar characters. Those of peculiar religious views, refugees from every country, poor people glad of shelter, gathered there. It was the rendezvous of conspirators; and members of secret societies who led a thought-life, which stamped them dreamers in the eyes of the world. All confided their ambitions and aspirations to Mazaro, believing him in sympathy with them, whereas he merely studied them as the scientist does his subject. Artists were delighted with the picturesque ruins and quaint old art gallery, containing works by masters long forgotten. There were rooms representing every nation. The one containing ivories was, perhaps, the most interesting, telling the sad tale of human brutality and savagery. Mazaro's immense wealth and old title gave him place in the highest circles of society. His visits there, however, were not returned save when some *debutante* or distinguished stranger was introduced. It was a like occasion that caused a company of the artistic world to pass through the gates one morning in early summer.

The opening of the theatrical court in the palace, unused since the days when the stage was under royal patronage, gave an additional interest to this occasion. The rays of the afternoon sun fell aslant the court that had been almost transformed into an Egyptian temple. On either side of the stage, open to the sky, sat a sphinx. Music faint and low vibrated in the temple. Mazaro appeared, leading Zulona. Her jewels flashed with a strange brilliancy; the drapery about her head intensified the expression of her eyes till she seemed a sorceress. Had the sphinx revealed to her the Great Problem?

She speaks. Her deep tones, soft, sweet, flute-like, float through the court. The voice is the same that rivaled the birds on Tehuacana Hills.

The words uttered, are a fitting accompaniment to the surroundings.

"This great philosophy is based upon man's being. The expression of this nature comprises the whole sum of life—expression so replete no man comprehends."

In a lengthy discourse, spoken in a language which she enunciated with a faint, foreign accent, she told of man's enchainment, and how he might be released.

The musician, the sculptor, the painter, the actor, the poet, learned that every sound, motion, form and attitude have their meaning, more definite and complete than words. The reason was given for their inherent and conventional meaning.

Then came the relation of these to their counterpart, that made the musician listen breathlessly.

The music echoes through the ruins of the palace. It steals through the court. Zulona's body sways and moves with a rhythm mesmeric. The music grows stronger, the motion becomes more complex. One need not be told it expresses all the passions; he sees, feels, lives them with her. Now, she is a village maiden waiting for a lover, and as easily becomes a Cleopatra reclining on a luxurious couch, surrounded by slaves. The transition from anger to horror, from terror to ecstasy and insanity, is made with lightning-like rapidity. She seems Tragedy incarnate—an infuriated goddess, an Amazon, and suddenly Medusa stares beneath the short curls that are living snakes, moving and coiling about her head. When she reaches ecstasy, a shiver runs through the audience; her eyes glare in insanity, the fillet is torn from her hair, that falls in waves over the shoulders. With a sudden movement, the arm is drawn above the face; crouching, she leers at them through the gold veil.

Then, like a broken flower, she droops, sinks lower, and swoons beside the sphinx.

CHAPTER ELEVENTH.

> "Come ye near unto me, hear ye this; I have not spoken in secret from the beginning; from the time that it was, there am I: and now the Lord God, and his Spirit, hath sent me."
> Isaiah, Chap. 47, 16th verse.

At the gates of the Strange Palace, Garangula stood waiting; in his countenance that mysterious look, indefinable, save to those who live the faith-life.

Since early dawn he had stood there. By-and-by, the servants assembled in the grounds, awaiting the arrival of the guests. Mazaro walked down the broad avenue to give the signal for the opening of the gates.

His eyes fell upon Garangula, who entered as the gates opened. Garangula crossed his hands on his breast and said, "O, Chief of this dwelling-place! Garangula, the Indian, seeks the beautiful pale-face."

"What pale-face seekest thou, O, handsome Garangula," inquired Mazaro, adopting the Indian's manner of speech.

"Dost thou not know? She is the child of the sun. Her eyes are stars. She moves like the wild animals on the plains."

Mazaro was a man who thought rapidly, planned as he thought, and executed without delay.

"Zulona—?" said he.

"The star-eyed pale-face," Garangula replied.

Mazaro had never before seen a man who so typified the ideal of masculine grace, as Garangula. Mazaro loved the beautiful regardless of what it expressed. He would make himself the owner of Garangula, as he would of a sleek and graceful animal. The companion that he wanted, was not so much for thoughts of the soul as for sensuous beauty. He had traveled the world over to find a human specimen, that he could cage or caress at his pleasure. Zulona was at the Palace; she was beautiful; her voice was liquid music; Mazaro could feast his eyes and his ears; but he was not a voluptuary; his adoration of beauty was objective and not subjective. Could he have retained the beautiful, without the individual, he would have done so. Garangula was beautiful; he desired to keep him, now that he was within the Palace gates. But Garangula should not see the "star-eyed pale-face"; he should have no object to attract his attention; with the impassiveness of an idol, Garangula should receive Mazaro's adoration. His eyes rested on Garangula's face, with a satisfied look.

"She is not here," he said.

Garangula looked at him a moment and said, "The Star-Eyed-One tarries in the great dwelling-place. Garangula will see her."

Mazaro lowered his eyes; he felt baffled, and yet, not one moment would he yield.

"Ah, well, stay here until you find her; she may be in some neighboring villa."

"Garangula will abide here until he find her," the Indian replied.

Mazaro beckoned to his slaves. "Lead on

to the royal apartments," he said, speaking in a language unknown to Garangula. "Serve this man as though standing before a prince—give him wine and fruits, burn incense; sing with the harp, dance; anything, everything that will engage him."

A few hours later, he found the Indian listening to the slaves singing their native songs; apparently he understood them. Mazaro ordered a repast, himself eating little, while he talked to his guest.

In all great situations, in everything that Mazaro felt deeply, he manifested the greatest indifference. He told story after story, and Garangula listened with simple, child-like pleasure; but at the end, said, "Garangula wishes to see the star-eyed pale-face."

Mazaro almost gave vent to his annoyance; but he answered quietly, with his most persuasive smile, "Let me show you the grounds, forests I should say, of the Strange Palace. You will see animals, birds, fishes, reptiles of every kind."

Garangula's delight was boundless as they wandered through the grounds. He seemed to have forgotten his quest. When evening was come, they entered the banquet-hall. It was an odd fancy of Mazaro to conceal his identity from his guests, having it announced that the master was away. It pleased him to do so that evening, doubtless that his entire time might be given to Garangula. He linked his arm in that of the Indian, and together they moved among the guests, who already talked as friend to friend. There were brilliant spaces of light in different parts of the hall, and yet no lights were visible. Within these spaces were reflected the table service of precious metals, the flowers, the servants as they moved noiselessly over the marble floor. This, and the incongruity of the guests, the subdued music of the band, the dancing of maidens upon a plateau not far away, made a scene that strangely moved Garangula.

The spaces of light grew more and more brilliant, the music stronger, the dancing wilder. Mazaro, forgetting that he had desired to remain *incognito*, emptied his cup of wine, and cried:

"Oh life, thou art beauty: thy beginning, aim, and end.... beauty. There is naught else."

And looking at Garangula, he said: "And thou, oh, Child of the Woods, art all I have ever dreamed that life could be! Thou art so beautiful! Leave me not! Leave not this Palace, and I will abide here forever. Knowest thou not," he drew closer and whispered, "I can teach thee to live always, to keep thy beauty as it now is?"

The Indian answered, his voice like the echo of angels' songs, "O Star-Eyed-One, Garangula seeks thee."

CHAPTER TWELFTH.

> "He was a man, take him for all in all, I shall
> not look upon his like again."
> Shakespeare.

It was a fortnight after Garangula reached the Strange Palace, and he had not seen Zulona. Hundreds of people had paid tribute to her genius—she had suddenly become one of the celebrities of the world. The Indian had been near her many times; but thus far, Mazaro had accomplished his design.

They were in the Jewel Chamber, its wonders being rivaled only by the Tosha'khanas in the courts of India. The floor was inlaid with cut stones of fabulous value; the ceiling and walls were covered with jewels. In the ceiling were radiating suns of amber. The

Indian looked in breathless wonder. After a long time he said, "They are sounds of spirits on their way to the Happy Hunting-Grounds."

Mazaro abruptly left the Jewel Chamber, saying, under his breath, "Now comes the last test. If he pass this, I fear to lose him."

"Do you love serpents?" he asked.

"Garangula loves all things."

"We shall see, we shall see," said Mazaro, smiling, not entirely with pleasure. They suddenly came upon a den of snakes. "Look for your life!" Mazaro spoke to a tall, thin, wiry-looking man who stood at the entrance.

"This man goes in there, stays three hours, and comes out alive! Comes out alive, or your head! Hear you?"

The man bowed low.

They looked through the opening at the snakes.

"Are you willing to go in there and touch that you claim to love?" Mazaro asked.

"Garangula will go."

Mazaro turned pale. Fearing to show his feelings, he said, "Enter," and turned away.

The gate opened, and Garangula stood within the gloomy den of serpents hissing, coiling and creeping among each other. Suddenly a ray of light broke through the gloom; the serpents ceased to move. The light grew and filled the den. Garangula stepped among the serpents and put his hands caressingly upon their heads; the light grew stronger. Garangula lifted his face toward the ceiling; it was radiant, his eyes became fixed, his lips moved.

"Great Spirit! O Holy Light!" he breathed.

CHAPTER THIRTEENTH.

"Now is the winter of our discontent made glorious summer by this sun of York—"
Shakespeare.

THE twilight stole through the stained windows of the Egyptian Apartments occupied by Zulona. Why she should have been given these, no one but Mazaro, knew. A soft, seductive poetry filled the rooms—Zulona, robed as a princess, half reclined on a tiger-skin. She was an Egyptian to-night; to-morrow she might be Russian or German, but now she was a daughter of the Nile: the pyramids might claim her for aught one knew. Her eyes expressed wonder and the green in them was deeper. Whether this were acting, or another phase of her character, none could tell.

Rachel held Wanda, whose lids drooped lower and lower as she sang a soft lullaby. Dixie, the dog, his big head on his paws, barked 'in his dreams. Aunt Dinah was seated on a high stool, the legs of which were crossed and mounted with three falcon heads holding the leather seat in their beaks. She was a quaint picture of reposeful serenity, mentally congratulating herself on the warmth that "cum frum she didn't know whar, but it wus mighty nice ter be alluz cumftible widout trouble."

Aunt Dinah was devotedly attached to Zulona, whom she had nursed from babyhood. "Ole Dinah don't see many like her now-a-days," she often said, "and she's gwine ter follow dis one 'tel dese ole bones am laid to res'. 'Taint gwine ter be long, an' ole Dinah would be willin' ter go ef she could see her boy dat wuz taken away, long time ago. I wonder ef I'll see my chile dis side de grave."

When it was grown dark, Zulona said: "Oh, Aunt Dinah, do sing one of your old songs.

I always want them when I feel sad; I think I shall wish to hear one when I'm dying."

Aunt Dinah began rocking herself to and fro, and humming in a low voice, the mournful cadences floating among the shadows of the room. Then came the words clear and triumphant.

" 'Moses smote de water,
　　An' de sea gabe away;
De chillun dey crossed ober,
　　An' de sea gabe away.
Oh! Lawd, I feel so glad,
　　It am always dark fo' day,
So honey don't you be sad,
　　De sea'll gib away—
　　De sea'll gib w–a–y!' "

The tones died away in thrilling sadness. Wanda suddenly opened her eyes, raised herself, and looked. Dixie moved, then bounded from the room. A moment later, he proudly returned, looking back with many extra wags of his tail. Aunt Dinah leaned forward with a frightened look—she was always on the alert in the Strange Palace. Zulona changed to a more indolent and graceful attitude—Garangula stood before her.

Zulona slowly rose and extended her hand. "Garangula!" she said.

The Indian bowed his head and crossed his hands on his breast. "Star-Eyed-One, Garangula, the Indian, greets thee." Then bending over Wanda he touched her cheek caressingly, "Little papoose.....Little pale-faced papoose!"

Aunt Dinah crouched away in a corner saying, under her breath, "Bress de Lawd! Ole Dinah purty nigh skeered ter def. How did dat Injun git here? Feel like I'm a-lookin' at er real live ghost dis time—guess ole Dinah's gittin' paid back fur declarin' she's seen so many befo'. De white folks feels strange, too, 'bout it, but dey won't show it," and she looked at Zulona with increasing admiration.

A servant in livery entered, bearing on a jeweled salver, the compliments of Mazaro. Having been ushered in with great ceremony, Mazaro said to Zulona, "I have been thinking perhaps you might have friends whom you would like to invite to the Palace. Pray consider them welcome. The rooms looking toward the East, are at your disposal."

From his manner toward Garangula, one could not judge whether he had seen him before.

As Mazaro left the room he said, in a low, resolute voice, "I will bide my time. He shall come to me some day; it may be many years, but it shall be—it shall be. I will bide my time."

Having determined on a certain result, Mazaro never gave it up. When baffled, he bore it seemingly without feeling, and to the casual observer, might have been turned from his course; but in his will there was never one moment of wavering—in his most trivial hours he thought and planned for the end in view. He never made one move that was not in that direction, though it appeared he went in a thousand diverse paths. That he did not always accomplish his designs, was fate, not Mazaro's fault. He held no further communication with Garangula during his stay in the Strange Palace, though he was cognizant of every movement and almost every word.

"This Palace is not mine, but I reside here at present, and offer thee hospitality, even as thou didst me on the plains," said Zulona to the Indian.

"Garangula will stay," he replied.

"Bress de Lord!" exclaimed Aunt Dinah. "He gwine ter stay here, too! Well, so long as dat purty white creetur am here ole Dinah'll be. It beats me how dat Injun frum Texas got here, an' he neber bin enny whar but on de ranch, an' he cum in jes' as home-like as ef he'd ben a-walkin' in dem wigwums on de hills. He needn't be a-comin' ter see my purty mistiss, though she do look at him powerful concarned like," she whispered to Rachel.

CHAPTER FOURTEENTH.

> "This above all—to thine own self be true;
> And it must follow, as the night the day,
> Thou canst not then be false to any man;
> Farewell; my blessing season this in thee."
> Shakespeare..

It did not occur to Garangula anyone would wonder about his coming. He wished to see the "pale-face," and left his home believing he would find her. It was a very simple thing to do what one wished. The Great Spirit would guide his children, if they would be led. His mother had taught him that the white man reasoned and studied—that was why he often lost his way. The influence of this teaching had remained undisturbed by Lord Carleton—the English lord—of whom Garangula had spoken to Zulona. Ah, Lord Carleton! Garangula thought of him even now, as he stood before Zulona. Lord Carleton, while on his ranch in Texas, not only had shared his rude cabin with the Indian, but had conceived a great affection for the mild-mannered son of the forest. He taught and loved Garangula as a younger brother. They were both noblemen, of different races. Lord Carleton often said, "I have never known a soul so grand, a character so simple. I love him more than a brother."

He had carefully invested Garangula's money, not a small sum of which had been left him by his father. He had looked forward to the time when he would take him to England; in truth, he had pictured their future together.

A few days after Zulona had left Tehuacana Hills, Garangula appeared before Lord Carleton, prepared for a journey, saying, "Garangula goes to seek the star-eyed pale-face. He knows not whither she has gone, or how long she may tarry. But he knows he will find her."

A frank soul spoke from his dark eyes that had in their depths calm resolution.

Lord Carleton uttered a low exclamation.

Here was a dilemma—what could be done? He knew full well it would be impossible to dissuade him. He heard the cowboys discussing the wonderful appearance of some ladies camping out, and thought this most extraordinary and not altogether in good form, but he had learned, immediately upon his arrival, that American women had more independence of character than those of any other nation, and less regard for conventionalities—a trait he did not admire in the least—and his curiosity was in no wise awakened until Garangula described them. Then he went to see them, but they had gone. He had not spoken to Garangula of their departure—he could not have told why; the subject had been a disagreeable one from the first. Now, he was going to seek her. If he only knew more of this woman who had robbed him of Garangula's companionship! Who was she? What was her influence over Garangula? It could not be for good—such a woman! Perhaps he would not find her—this thought brought little comfort.

"Shall I tell him of conventional life?" he

thought. "No, no, I could never make him understand. I wonder if there be a woman on God's earth, that would play with his heart? If so, heaven help him!"

Garangula stood child-like, unable to understand Lord Carleton's sadness. Childlike as the Indian of old, he thought nothing of the expenses of the journey. He had put together his Indian costumes and carried them as his forefathers had done. He was going to seek the "star-eyed" woman. That was all. Why did the English lord look sorrowful?

These Indian costumes he loved; it was not vanity that prompted this, but the barbaric love of ornament that belongs to the savage, and the intense love of the beautiful inseparable from the exalted soul. He would have decorated anything that belonged to him. His usual dress was a curious blending of the Oriental with that of the primitive Indian of North America. Lord Carleton had wondered at the Oriental touches till Garangula told him he once found some pictures in his father's books, and was so pleased with them his mother said she could make him look as those people. She had woven into them, however, much of her own barbaric taste, and Garangula still adhered to the old custom of Indian ornaments and skins.

The morning of his departure, Garangula threw the deer-skin over his shoulder as he entered Lord Carleton's door. His face was illumined with intuitive light.

"By Jove!" exclaimed Lord Carleton, "how like a god you look!" Then mentally, "What a sensation he would create in a London drawing-room!"

He was sorely perplexed, notwithstanding, when Garangula stood firm in his resolution to seek the beautiful pale-face in that dress. Finding all efforts unavailing, he looked at his attire, worn with such becoming dignity, and said:

"After all, you could wear nothing else."

Going to a box, the lid of which was not secured by a lock — locks are unnecessary in Texas — he took some gold and a large roll of bank notes, and gave them to Garangula.

"Good-by, and the Great Spirit bless you. When you have found the star-eyed pale-face, write me. You can write well enough for me to understand."

After Garangula had gone, Lord Carleton found the evenings at the Ranch very dull. Formerly, they were spent in teaching his protégé, giving him sketches of travel, or reading from the poets, while Garangula listened intently, interrupting to ask what certain passages meant, then telling the thoughts that came to him. They were always original, and often, even more poetical, Lord Carleton thought, than those they had been reading. He marveled much at Garangula's way of expressing himself, until one day, he told him that his father "had many books and knew great learning."

"Then I wonder you never learned to read," Lord Carleton rejoined.

"Garangula's mother would never consent to that. She let his father talk to him and teach him the white man's speech, and Garangula remembers that at times he talked like the English lord. Then again, in a strange language he spoke, and said it was that of his own people."

"Try to recall some words of the strange language," said Lord Carleton, eagerly; he had long wished to know to what nation Garangula's father belonged.

"Garangula cannot. His mother begged that her child should not learn it. 'Books were the cause of all the trouble in the world,' she said. Garangula shall never study books; it would make his mother unhappy. Why should men learn books, when the Great Spirit has given them so many other ways to read?"

Lord Carleton had been very careful about what he read to Garangula—that which would enlarge his poetic nature, but always avoided telling him of the white man's religion, wishing him to keep his simple faith in the Great Spirit.

A fortnight after Lord Carleton had bidden good-by to Garangula, he had a note from him dated "New York," that is, the postmark on the envelope was such.

"By Jove! Going across the sea! Is the boy mad? Why did I not remonstrate with him, beg him never to leave me?"

But there was a quiet dignity about the Indian that silenced interference.

That evening, Lord Carleton sat thinking of his friend more and more regretfully. How he missed him!

"Going across the sea to seek the pale-face! Will he find her? Will he make his way in the world? I have often thought of the strange manner in which he came to me. There he stood by the doorway, and said, 'Garangula, the Indian, is lonely in the wigwam on the hillside. His mother is gone. May he abide with thee?'

"I looked at him a moment; his great soul went out to mine. I clasped his hand and gave him welcome. I, too, was lonely, and my heart warmed to this simple child of nature. How I have guarded him! As closely perhaps, as the Indian mother, who seemed to live in constant dread lest her child should be contaminated by the white man. Many nights, when it was necessary for him to be with the herds, have I taken a blanket and lain on the ground by his side. There we would lie, looking up at the stars and the lamp of the Great Spirit, and talk about the Happy Hunting-Grounds—I, often falling asleep with his musical voice sounding faintly in my ears. But when necessity did not compel, I kept the Indian with me in the evening—those blessed evenings!"

Many thoughts chased each other through his mind, but among all, Garangula was foremost.

When he arose, Lord Carleton had formed new plans, which he was unable to execute for a long time.

CHAPTER FIFTEENTH.

> "Watch ye, and keep them until ye weigh them before the chief of the priests and the Levites, and chief of the fathers of Israel at Jerusalem, in the chambers of the House of the Lord."
>
> Ezra, viii. 29.

A DUSKY face looked from the window of an institution devoted to the education of the Indian race. The building was surrounded by trees and a garden that stretched toward one of the gently sloping hills covered with blue grass.

The dark eyes gazed wistfully at the trees and sky.

"Oh, trees, and hills, and stream, talk to me!" she cried. "Many times has the moon hung above me since I have dwelt here. Garangula called it 'the Lamp.' How strange was all he spoke! He called me 'noble maiden'—was

I not daughter of a chieftain? Long ago that seems. They call time by years here, and it is longer. The red man counts by the grass, and moon, and snows, and one grows not old. But tell it as may be, it is long since Garangula and I roamed together. His mother brought him to my tribe that he might know her race. He was one of us, and still unlike us. Only twelve winters had passed o'er him, yet when he spoke my people listened. Ofttimes he talked to the rocks, and trees and birds. One night—the lamp in the sky burned brighter than now—I was awakened by Garangula. 'See! See!' he cried. When I asked him what it was, he said: 'Garangula believes they are the people who make the forests and all there is in them. Look! Look! They touch the large rock, and it moves. They are dancing above the flowers. Beautiful! Beautiful!' He clasped his hands and spoke no more. Soon his eyes closed and he slept, but I sat there looking straight into the forest trying to see 'the people'; sat there till the birds sang in the morning. Their songs brought me no gladness, for Garangula's mother would set out on her return when the sun rose in the heavens.

"A long time after, did Leota, the Indian maiden, look in the woods for 'the people'. Then did the faithful Noncuso go to bring news of Garangula. And this word he brought—'Garangula dwells with a white man who owns many herds. The white man teaches Garangula from books.'

"The Indian maiden went to the pale-face who had come to teach her people, and begged to be sent where she, too, might learn from books. The grass has been long growing, the birds slow in building their nests, but the Indian maiden has been faithful. Some time Garangula and she may meet, and together help their people."

A deep sigh told the story of self-repression through an effort for abnormal development.

Her eyes flashed. She sprang up, tore the dark hair from its confinement, and unlaced her robe, standing with naught but a blanket about her. She drew a long, deep breath and held it—a luxury she had not known in her toilet of stays. She stretched herself to her full height, then drawing her blanket close, she leaped from the window, caught the branch of a tree, and sprang to the ground. At a bound she had left the garden and was gliding down the slope of the hill. In wild ecstasy she clasped a tree and talked to it in her own language. For a moment her body swayed to and fro, then in sheer abandonment she flung herself on the ground, and lay so still, her heart seemed to beat as one with the great earth....She arose—the rebellion and wildness had vanished. She moved down the valley where a stream laughed on its way, and sang and danced about it; then knelt and looked in the woods for "the people". After a time, the eyes drooped and she dreamed by the water. When the light from the east stole through the woods, the Indian maiden rose dumb with wonder; she shivered at the great unknown unfolding before her. Drawing her blanket close about the head, she leaned forward—the deep-set eyes looked out piercingly, striving to know as others have done. "The Indian maiden knows not the mystery! Leota understands not!".... she cried out.

The eyes ceased to wonder. She folded her arms across her breast and said: "O, Great Spirit, Leota, the Indian maiden, will go on."

The blanket fell from her form. A great light swept over her ...... "For Garangula's sake—for thy people—my people, Garangula. The Indian maiden cannot divide them. She loves one through the other. She loves both as one."

The light grew softer, her voice died away— "Spirit—Garangula—thy people—my people."

CHAPTER SIXTEENTH.

> "They have been at a great feast of languages,
> and stolen the scraps."
> *Shakespeare.*

THE fame of Zulona's lecture in the Strange Palace, spread afar. Many invitations followed. A most important one came from the Academy of Music, inviting her to speak; especially did the opera singers wish to hear the laws of song expounded. When learning this, Mazaro said: "Go not; I will invite them to come here. Take my advice—be great enough to draw the world to you. Of course, there are people who must seek, but it is far greater to be sought."

It was arranged the Academy of Music should hold its next convention within the Strange Palace. There was great excitement among the members. If the Prophetess—as she was called—set forth the truths some were led to think, she might create a School of Art.

A new era seemed dawning, and the hope of deliverance from shackles at hand. The season of the Capital was not over, and many social stars were among the audience that day.

When Zulona entered the theatre a message was placed in her hands. She gave it a glance and staggered; but by the time she had reached the stage, her emotion was mastered, and she smiled gratefully at the applause which greeted her.

"The great Master of whom I shall tell you, said, 'Art is feeling passed through thought and fixed in form.' Thus Art sweeps the whole realm of being and has the same underlying principles that life has. And since it doth not yet appear what man shall be, there is no limit to art, so far as our present vision can discern. And, furthermore, since the Universal is inexhaustible, it must be believed with a holy faith, that every man has an individuality to express."

She classified the different Schools of Art, beginning with the earliest. She illustrated each school so forcefully, the audience felt awed at her power. They realized the influence of her magnetism. "She is an adept in occult science and is casting a spell over her audience," some declared.

Perhaps both. Was it done with understanding? Opposition gives dignity, grandeur—tragedy. Parallelism is a symbol of equality, universal brotherhood. He who understands the application of these, knows the relation between good and evil.

The audience began to wonder how one so young, could have reached such heights.

She paused a moment, then concluded: "My Master gave his life to the study of Man's being, the true knowledge of which, is the basis of the Artistic School. He studied in hospitals, asylums, among the poor, the great—everywhere, that he might teach the Expression of Humanity. I will not picture to you the details of his struggles. His life-work has ceased. I have in my hand this mournful message: '*The Master hath gone from us.*'

"Yesterday the world was rich—he lived; today the world is poor—doubly poor, because it recognized not what it possessed. He lived before his time, as do all great souls. Many sat at his feet and drank wisdom. He died in obscurity because he cared not for applause.

"'The people weep not, nor do they rise to build a monument to his memory. He needs it not. The time will come when you will say, 'Let us atone for the past! Let us honor him who has been among us! Let us make recompense.'

"Only by taking the truths he left you and making them known to the uttermost ends of the earth, may you atone. Had I the power to leave a memorial worthy of my Master, I should give you that for which he lived and worked— *Truth Immortal.*"

CHAPTER SEVENTEENTH.

> "I am Sir Oracle,
> And when I ope my lips, let
> no dog bark."
> Shakespeare.

GARANGULA, seated in the Royal box, presented a strange contrast to the fashionable audience. While influenced by the music of Zulona's voice, he was perplexed over her words. Classic, Romantic, and Artistic were to him unknown terms. This superb child of Nature could comprehend no School. It seemed strange that one had to exercise in order to make graceful movements. As to acting, he had never thought about it until now; but if he wished to play a part, he would know how. Did not the Great Spirit teach us all things?

While in New York, he went to the theatre where Edwin Forrest was playing Metamora. He depicted the character with such wonderful vividness, Garangula felt he was looking at his forefathers. It was so natural to Indian life that he did not question; he could not understand it was acting.

He lived again scenes he witnessed when his mother took him to the Indian camps. He saw the wigwams as the light shone on them from the camp-fires. His mother's tribe gathered around them singing songs and dancing; the bright red costumes, the feathers in their hair, the beads flashing in and out, made glowing pictures by the fire-light. A successful chieftain returned to his camp, the scalps of his victims hanging to his belt, the dancers around him venting their savage delight in Indian yells. They ate their supper of venison and Indian corn, and the war-dance began, as the climax of the play was reached.

The evening after the lecture, Zulona said: "Will Garangula learn of me?"

"He will listen to the star-eyed pale-face. She will be kind like the English lord."

Zulona desired him for a pupil because his movements had in them a promise of something that even she felt would be difficult to acquire.

Many times she said, "The artist can be created."

"Granted," replied another. "True unfoldment would make every man an artist. But how few understand what Unfoldment means. No man is greater than another. The seeming difference lies in the fact that some are free and some are slaves. There is a Philosophy, if comprehended, that would enable every man to shake off the chains and unfold the poetry in his soul. Like the Star of old, it shineth from afar. Its rays are beginning to pierce the mists of this life. He who would become a great artist, must receive its light."

Nothing so angered Zulona as a supposition of art knowledge on the part of another. In this realm she reigned alone, and would not brook contradiction. Her temper once given vent to, she expressed herself in immoderate terms. Her words were nothing, however, compared to the mobility of her face. She hissed with her lips and cursed with her eyes.

This woman so radiantly beautiful, acknowledged no higher expression in nature than the human, accepted no religion but Art—her presentation of it. When with her, one was almost persuaded to her interpretation of Expression, she was so perfect in beauty.

Her motion was entrancing. It was this, more than her beauty of face and form that made men her worshipers. When acting, this motion was anything from dreams of angels to the angles of discordant demons.

She gave her powers full range as she hurled sentence after sentence at a recent criticism on her art, attacking what she considered her beliefs. She scorned it as unworthy of an artist, defying the verification in either Art or life.

But when she turned to Garangula, a fascinating smile lighted her face; she said:

"That philosophy of which I am a follower, is high as heaven. deep as hell. The eternal truths uplift it. Through its influence, gods and goddesses, as heretofore, will walk the earth."

The Indian arose with a wonderful expression on his face, and said:

"O, Star-Eyed-One, Garangula will sit at thy feet and gain wisdom, but the beautiful pale-face will pardon Garangula if he beg her not to teach him what she has been saying. He will do whatever the Great Spirit that dwells in here"—he had laid his hand on his breast—"whatever the Great Spirit tells him, but he cannot learn of other things."

Zulona's face was as difficult to define as that of Garangula. At last she extended her hand to him, and said: "You may learn as you like. Let us begin."

She gave a gymnastic of the arms. Garangula watched her a moment, then raised his arms slowly, and with perfect rhythm made the motion indicated.

Finding she could teach him nothing in this preliminary drill, she told him to improvise in gesture, and explained what she meant.

No words can describe Garangula's wonderful improvisation.

The first scene was a young Indian fighting against the white man for his bride. He held his ground calmly till the whites rushed on him, then he looked like a wild animal at bay. He pushed his bride behind him, and with one more struggle, which proved futile, turned suddenly, clasped her in his arms, and leaped from the cliff.

Then came a Chieftain in battle. He looked a giant as he stood calm and fearless among his enemies, his head thrown haughtily back, scorn pictured on his countenance, his eyes aglow with superhuman courage. This increased as his comrades fell around him and the enemy drew nigh. At length, they closed upon him. Then followed the most superb natural acting perhaps ever witnessed. He towered like a great mountain whose every crevice and peak are seen in the glaring sunlight, but over which no mist hangs to give ideality and poetry.

The time came when he must yield. He

bared his breast and fell forward without a groan.

From these scenes he drifted into others, wherein one saw more clearly than before, the influence of Lord Carleton. He was improvising from the poetry that had been read to him, and it was remarkable how he gave a certain *finesse* to the characters, that was wholly wanting in the first acting, a few artistic touches here and there, that were a marked contrast to the romantic, rugged impersonations of Indian life, that inspired one with such fire and enthusiasm.

But so far, he had done nothing original; he had merely copied in a marvelous manner that which he either witnessed or had been described to him by his mother, and the pictures that had remained with him from the Englishman's reading. It was beautiful; nay, it was wonderful; but was it creative? Was he an artist? As one watched this Indian, he began asking for the first time, Should one study art? And is it true that every man is a poet? If so, then it is also true that civilized man has drifted so far from the child of nature, he must spend years finding his way back.

For on one point there is no question—*No civilized man expresses himself.*

WE ARE ALL LIARS.

CHAPTER EIGHTEENTH.

> "I talk of dreams;
> Which are the children of an idle brain;
> Begot of nothing but vain phantasy;
> Which is as thin of substance as the air;
> And more inconstant than the winds,
> Who woos even now, the frozen bosom of the north,
> And being anger'd, puffs away from thence,
> Turning his face to the dew—dropping south."
> Shakespeare.

> "For God speaketh once, yea twice, yet man perceiveth it not."
> Job xxxiii. 14.

"God offers to everyone his choice. I have chosen to seek the truth, and he who seeks, has no rest. I cannot understand how all my earnest efforts have failed. Oh, God, help me!" she cried out in anguish. "All things have failed to bring me to the light. My last hope was this beautiful art. I had faith in it, I thought it contained the Philosophy of Life. I have studied faithfully for years. It has thrown light on the way, yes, much light. There are many things I see clearly that were dark before, and I vaguely wonder sometimes, if, when I have fully mastered it, I shall not have the whole truth. I still have hope at times, and through this, continue the struggle. Would not a man who was complete master of the whole circle of art and science, be a harmonious man? But I feel so far from grasping it as a whole. I think the fault mine; I feel in some way I am not seeking aright—I know its end is peace. Alas! I am growing more unhappy each day, more discordant every hour. No man has reached the truth until he become harmonious in body, mind, and soul. I cannot believe the invalid, however patient and resigned, is within the pale of Truth.

"I talk of Truth, and I realize not what it is. I feel to-day that I do not even know what I am seeking. I am all astray—longing, longing for something.

"What is Truth? Who knows? I thought for a time it meant culture, that he who had the highest culture, was nearest the Truth.

"Perhaps there is much in this, but I have lived to know that the beggar by the roadside, who never heard the word 'culture', may be nearer the truth than many of the learned. Thus, many definitions have played me false, till I am now in the hopeless condition of knowing not for what I am struggling. And the pain here," she pressed her hands to her temples, "is growing harder to bear day by day, and with it a deep unrest has come. I have resolved to go away and live alone and find a philosophy of my own."

Aunt Dinah, who had been standing by the door, listening, looked at her wonderingly.

"What am you tryin' ter fin', Miss Rachel? You ain't lost dat purty brespin you wears, is yer?"

Rachel smiled faintly in spite of her weariness.

"No, Aunt Dinah, but I have had a dream that made me unhappy, even more so than I was before."

"Hope 'taint a bad un—tell me 'bout it," and Aunt Dinah seated herself preparatory to enjoying the dream. Next to ghost stories she liked dreams.

"This morning," said Rachel, "I felt too weary to study or work, so I laid down to rest, hoping I would fall asleep and forget my unhappy thoughts. Before I did this, I resolved I would go away for awhile, till I could get into a happier state."

"Law, Miss Rachel, what's de matter? Hab enny ob us hurt yo' feelin's? Ef it's ole Dinah she's ready ter ax yo' forgiveness right now."

"No, no, Aunt Dinah."

"Well, den, what is it? But tell me fust 'bout yo' dream."

"I thought," Rachel continued, " some one came to me and said: 'Yes, go your way, seclude yourself from the world and see if you can learn of Him who was meek and lowly, of Him *who ever went among his people doing good.* Try this, for it is one of the lessons you must learn.'

"Then, this being vanished, and all grew dark. I put out my hands trying to find the way, lest I fall into some treacherous abyss. I stumbled over sharp stones that cut my bare feet and left them bleeding and torn. I cried for help, but I heard no sound. I kept on the pathless track, growing more and more hopelessly lost. At last, I saw a narrow, winding path, but it was delusion; instead of nearing, I was getting further away from it, till I reached a spot where I was surrounded by a rugged cliff, whose sharp sides reached up to the heavens; by a thick woods, through which I could not see—and by a dark river, the foaming waters of which, rushed in front of me. There were long, forked tongues reaching out to draw everything within their fathomless depths. I shuddered and would have turned away, but my eyes became riveted on what at first appeared to be a mere speck; something compelled me to look

"I discovered that it was a small boat being tossed about by the waves that laughed in their demoniacal glee, as it became a mere plaything for their sport. I gradually saw the figure of a human being with his hands clutching the sides of the boat. At first, I thought he was alone, but after a time, I could see another figure at the prow of the boat. This did not appear human, but more like a Death's head. I could not shut out the sight. In a sepulchral voice, the Death's head said: 'You made your own choice. No one ever reaches the other side of these waters. You are nearing the spot where you will be drawn into its depths.'

"Then, with a look of terror that made my heart stand still, this human being, I could not tell if it were man or woman, rose and pleaded for mercy. The Death's head raised its long, skeleton hand, emphasizing its curse, as a mighty wave swept over both."

Aunt Dinah's eyes grew wider as Rachel continued: "With a cry of horror I turned and rushed to the foot of the cliff, and knelt praying I might be taken to the light once more. I was willing to climb up its steep, rugged sides—I was willing to walk in the highways and byways of men. As I knelt there, I heard a low, rumbling sound. It was faint and far-off, then it grew more and more distinct; a choking sensation came over me, the sounds were like roaring flames. I looked up. The cliff was on fire; the flames burst out in all their fury, gathering in strength and brilliancy from the centre. Oh, the glare of that burning cliff, illuminating the woods, underneath the thick, spreading branches of which, I could see the lairs of wild beasts! As the flames were enveloping me, a woman clothed in light appeared in the centre of the cliff. She rose as though borne upon wings, and floated through the flames till she reached the top, where she poised between earth and heaven.

"She looked down and smilingly reached out her hands towards me, then pointed to the forest. I looked, and lo! the woods were changed to a mighty city wherein men and women were struggling for life and happiness. Far down the street, a cathedral, whose spire touched the heavens, rose in solemn grandeur. Over this was a waning star, towards which the woman moved her arm in a spiral, looking upward. Then I heard a joyous burst of music."

"Dem wus de hebenly harps," said Aunt Dinah, confidently.

"I awoke," said Rachel, "to find it was only

the birds singing in the garden. The time was passing, and I was still slothful."

Aunt Dinah had been greatly interested in the dream, especially when the angel appeared, but now she observed Rachel more closely.

"Honey, you looks pale dis mornin'. What am de matter wid you, Miss Rachel, any how?"

"Oh, Aunt Dinah, I can't explain to you. I am trying to find the way—trying to learn how to do right."

A glad light broke over Aunt Dinah's face. "Now, honey, tell me, is you a mourner? Is you tryin' to git religion?"

Rachel smiled. "That is it, I suppose, Aunt Dinah."

"Bress de Lawd!" and she swayed her body, ready to start a genuine camp-meeting song. "Miss Rachel, what am you habin' all dis fuss 'bout it fur? Why don't you jes' drap right down on yo' knees and begin to pray? Jes' gib it all up to His ways."

"But how am I to know what are His ways, Aunt Dinah?"

"Law chile! Why jes' gib yersef right up

to Him. I wish you could hear some good ole preachin' I used ter hear way down de south. One preacher I member specially. He wus a curus lookin' man; he'd pulled de har offen his head when he'd be a studyin'. Dey said his wife had ter wrap his hands up ter keep him from pullin' it all clean out. His eyes sumetimes 'minded ole Dinah of live coals, and folks said he wuz purty nigh crazy, but I think he wuz de smartest man I eber see. One time he tole a story, it warn't no dream, nor story, nuther, it was so—it happened. He said: 'Once dar wuz a po' man a hangin' way up on a cliff, and he wuz 'bout ter fall, jes' a holdin' on ter some little saplin's, and ennything he could ketch, skeered too 'bout fallin', fur ef he fell he'd kill hisself, sho', case way down below him wuz so fur he couldn't see, and he'd strike his head 'gin de rocks, and lan', he didn't know whar. Jes' as he wuz 'bout ter fall, he looked up 'bove him—he wuz a prayin', I reckon, and he see a great white angel a hoverin' up above him, a shore nuff angel, wid great wings, an' he 'peared so strong an' so lovin'. He looked down on de man, sort of pityin' like, an' de man he looked back at him an' cried out: 'Help me! Sabe me!' De angel sort ob smiled lobinly an' said: 'Dust thou beliebe I kin sabe you?'

"An' de man said: 'Yes, I beliebe it.'

"Den de angel said: 'Are yer willin' ter be sabed?'

"De man wus 'bout fallin' by dis time and skeered purty nigh ter def, an' he knowed he couldn't sabe hisself, an' so he cried out mighty quick: 'Yes, I am willin' ter be sabed.'

"Den de angel smiled and said:

"'Let go.'"

CHAPTER NINETEENTH.

"Look here, upon this picture, and on this."
Shakespeare,

ONE evening, in the height of the autumn season, there was a gay assemblage of nobility in the brilliant drawing-rooms of the Strange Palace.

Drawing-room lectures were not then so fashionable, but Zulona's fame made them a success.

She chose for her theme, Sketches from Mythological lore. The passion and pathos with which she interpreted them, differed from anything heretofore given, but her speech was so forcible, and logical, and the imagery so brilliant, her auditors were charmed, if not convinced. When she had finished speaking, she wove the different characters into one story, singing the while in a low recitative. From these, she passed to portrayals with such realistic passion that strong-men shivered.

The Indian was present, but did not seem to understand the lecture, although he said the English lord read of like pictures many times.

Zulona's wit and brilliancy of repartee were as marked as her cleverness in lecturing. The gentlemen sometimes learned this, to their chagrin. "Her wit," to use the words of Blackmore, "was full of corners, strange, jagged, and uncomfortable."

She looked so young she appeared girlish, and was radiant with her triumph. She knew the lecture had made her the most brilliant success of the Capital. Her face rippled with smiles, now coquettish, then perfectly artless, charming, tantalizing. No one in the Strange Palace had seen her thus. She had many opposing elements in her nature, seeming contradictions, and yet these moods, if they might be so called, while never related to each other, were always in harmony with her. She was more honest than most people—she ever acted as she felt. And one had the faith that she lived up to her principles, though what they were he never knew.

A little incident occurred that proved her complexity of character, and also afforded much amusement.

The lecture was on "The Religion of Art." She illustrated by parallelisms in the spiritual realm, throwing so beautiful a devotion into the attitude, she looked one of Fra Angelica's saints. While thus, she felt the audience were either not in a mood, or incompetent to appreciate. The pose ended. Zulona leaned forward, and whispering to a clergyman, said: "Hell and damnation!"

CHAPTER TWENTIETH.

"For the body is not one member, but many."
Cor. 12-14.

ZULONA'S next lecture was on the Birth of the Opera, continuing its history to the present century.

The room in which she spoke, was paneled in yellow and gold, with a frieze of bronze poppies so exquisitely arranged that one felt the magic wand waving over him, and he drifted into the land of dreams — dreams wherein one heard music in the softly-flowing draperies, whose intricate designs and coloring were ever telling stories of some artist's life.

Zulona was robed in harmony with her surroundings. As she arose, her eye fell on a book lying upon the table. Her face lighted with pleasure—the book was "The Life of Edwin Forrest," by Wm. R. Alger.

"Ah," she said, "I will first read what Alger says on the Church and Stage. No one has written so well. Indeed, I think no one is so competent to discuss both subjects, as the author of this book."

With one hand resting on the page, she read in that perfectly modulated voice, the chapter all the world should know. The author clearly shows the origin of the stage, then the different steps it takes till it becomes an independent guild, declaring its freedom from the church and courts. Side by side, he carries the Church and Stage, showing the mission of each, how far both fall short of their mission, and why since their separation, there has ever been enmity between them.

Then in a lengthy discourse, emphasizing what she had read, the Prophetess advanced new thoughts on music, going into the mysteries of art, in a manner she had not been known to do before. It has been said of Goethe that "his penetration of every secret of the fine arts made him statuesque." It was true of Zulona. She gave hints and criticisms to the painter, the sculptor, the musician, the poet, all of whom declared they had received light. She resembled Goethe in many respects, yet one sometimes wondered if she perceived the highest, and if the doubt must be entertained of her "capacity of self-surrender to the moral sentiment."

CHAPTER TWENTY-FIRST.

> "O, she doth teach the torches to burn bright!
> Her beauty hangs upon the cheek of night
> Like a rich jewel in an Ethiop's ear,
> Beauty too rich for use, for earth too dear!"
> —Shakespeare.

ONE finds it difficult to analyze the Indian, so near to nature is he. When in Zulona's presence, Garangula seemed to think of her only, yet, appeared to forget her when interested in the many wonderful things of the Strange Palace. Often when entering the Egyptian Apartments, he would speak softly, "Garangula wonders if he will find the dwelling-place empty. O, pale-face, O, beautiful pale-face!" No look of uneasiness came, only an expression of deep faith, as he whispered: "The Great Spirit will lead Garangula to her."

Garangula never reasoned. The young Englishman had endeavored to cultivate that faculty, but he had given up in despair.

One day, in reply to something Zulona told him, he said: "Garangula felt that at the theatre."

"Yes," she answered, "but you did not know the reason you felt so. You could not have analyzed your feelings."

"Garangula does not wish that," he replied. "He feels. Is it not all? Garangula does not understand how one could reason about a feeling—" he hesitated a moment. Zulona looked at him strangely.

"But, Garangula, I wish you would ask me reasons concerning the principles I advance. Who knows what you may be in the future? Perhaps you may have need of them."

"Garangula cannot think the time will ever come when he shall wish to know the reason for anything. When a truth is given him, he either knows it or he does not know it."

His lessons in Art continued, if lessons they could be called.

Zulona had never known so interesting a pupil, and yet so difficult to teach. A subject had to be presented to him in a certain way and form, and these were quite different from anything she had hitherto undertaken. There were many times when he did not seem to comprehend her meaning, yet looked at her so earnestly, that she said: "I believe Garangula does understand the truths I tell him. That double consciousness, which everyone possesses, is more highly developed in him, or rather it has not been educated out of him, and I seem to be looking through one, and speaking to the other that understands all."

On one occasion, she presented a formula that perplexed him; he arose and said: "Garangula feels his mother would not be pleased for him to listen to the beautiful pale-face to-day," and left the room.

It was one of his peculiarities not to exchange a greeting or farewell On entering a room he spoke his thoughts, and they were often the same the people were discussing. His exit was as unconventional as his entrance.

After one of his lessons, he turned when he had reached the door and said: "O Lady, thou art beautiful like the trees and clouds and stars."

Notwithstanding Garangula's many words of like manner, she was puzzled to understand him. Many of her followers loved her wildly, passionately, and she scarcely gave them a thought; but this Indian interested her. His very frankness baffled her, so little had the world in common with him.

Zulona's success and popularity in society was unquestioned; she held brilliant receptions in the Egyptian Apartments. This made a great difference in the peaceful life of Aunt Dinah, who, regardless of the confusion in the Strange Palace, moved along quiet ways, reposeful as only her race can be; happy in knowing her mistress was admired by the greatest of the world. But soon foreign domestics were sent to Zulona, and Aunt Dinah felt her reign was well-nigh ended. She longed more and more to find her son.

Wanda still mourned for Rachel's gentle touch and song.

The first Reception Zulona gave, she invited Garangula to be present. He soon became the cynosure of all eyes. The ladies raved over his handsome face and figure, and, stranger than all, they accepted his dress, which had been modified only a trifle. It was noticeable that the gentlemen present looked tame and commonplace beside that regal child of nature, who remained true to himself with a quiet dignity that charmed all. Their dress seemed ugly in contrast with his, which though wild and picturesque had nothing of the buccaneering appearance.

Garangula would have been unrelated to the ordinary costume of the day. Be it said to the credit of the civilized man, that much as he may have degenerated from the simplicity of olden times, he has not retrograded so far as to be in harmony with the dress he now wears.

The dress of woman has many faults, but it must be confessed it has in it some of the elements of beauty, entirely wanting in that of man.

Garangula's frankness and native costume were inseparable.

Zulona was as unconventional as Garangula, and was not disconcerted in the least, when Garangula said to a lady to whom he had just been presented: "Thou art like the flowers by the roadside where Garangula has knelt. He has looked into their hearts and they have talked back to him. Wilt thou, too, answer his words of love?" His eyes turned toward Zulona, and he said: "O, Star-Eyed-One, the Great Spirit has been kind to lead Garangula amid so much beauty."

By this time, Garangula and his companion were the observed of all. Some were shocked; one duchess nearly fainted, and had to be led from the room, but Garangula stood there, serene and unconscious, giving similar words to all; and truth, as it ever does, won the day. The ladies, when leaving, declared to their hostess she had the most charming guest they had ever known. The gentlemen expressed their regrets at not having been born a savage.

The day following, Zulona was reading a

poem, illustrating by allegorical gestures. Garangula threw his head back, closed his eyes, then gently opened them in the attitude of ecstasy......All was still ......Colors floated through the room......

Garangula opened his eyes, arose, and said: "Thy voice, O Lady, is like the colors surrounding thee."

Instantly the tones changed; she hastily took up Shelley's poems and read. Finishing, she threw the book aside, and said: "It is of no consequence whether there is a God or not."

A shadow passed over Garangula's face. He said: "Garangula must stand under the open sky."

Softly, mysteriously, a voice stole on the air: "Never has an artist denied God. For him, Art is still a mystic fountain from which flows celestial perfume, and through which he feels, he sees, he touches his God, and is filled with irrepressible raptures."

CHAPTER TWENTY-SECOND.

> "Wherefore I say unto thee, Her sins, which are many, are forgiven; for she loved much: but to whom little is forgiven, the same loveth little."
> Luke 7. 47.

RACHEL had found her retreat from the haunts of men—a seclusion the Sacred Brotherhood might envy. On one side, were the sea and beetling cliffs; from the other, the land stretched away in smiling downs and sunny uplands. The world had not yet reached that spot. No boats ever landed on the coasts, save a few wrecks washed there by the storms.

Rachel lay on the golden sands, watching the lights and shadows on the waters, the sails in the distance, the blue sky overhead.

"Surely," she said, "these are all sermons

for me. In every wave that touches the shore I hear the voice of God, but—afar off."

When the sea was stormy, and the waves beat wildly, till she could no longer listen, she walked in the quiet country lanes that whispered, "Peace!" Oh, the cool, shady, English lanes! The long lanes, bordered by fields of golden grain, the glowing sunsets, the slowly gathering twilight throwing shadows among the heavy, dark foliage of the trees, that rise sentinel-like along the way. Oh, the cool shadows of English lanes! The restful shadows! They come back to one in after years and soothe him.

Rachel was led to that beautiful spot, by her of the mysterious Light. There she found a home with an aged, childless couple, who soon learned to love Rachel as their own daughter, saying, "God has been good to send us this stray lamb." Rachel returned their affection with greater warmth than she displayed toward anyone save Wanda. It pleased them when she called them Uncle Jonah and Aunt Mary.

Uncle Jonah often walked not far behind, or

stood near Rachel when she climbed some cliff. "Lest harm might come to her" he would say. "Our old hearts would be sore indeed, for she looks so like the one we lost."

Three months had passed since Rachel went to the hermitage. One morning, she strolled along the sunny downs, her heart filled with the gladness around her. But as she walked on, the ever-vexed question arose in her mind. She did not speak her thoughts, but they filled her whole being. Suddenly she was startled by a voice saying: "Feed my lambs," and looked up to see a young artist sketching on the cliff in front of her.

"Yes, that is it—'Feed my lambs,'" he said again, without looking up from his work.

Rachel stopped; his words seemed strangely in answer to her question. As though impelled by some force, she went nearer, looked at him and said: "How could you know I was troubled with a question?"

He did not look around, but continued his strokes, as he said: "How did I know? How do we know anything?"

"How do we know anything?" Rachel repeated. "I am afraid I cannot tell; I had not thought much about it."

"Just so." He went a few steps from his picture to get a better view. "If that could have been solved as it will be some day, all the vexed questions would have been in their graves long ago."

"You talk like a philosopher," she said.

"I am," he replied, and resumed the use of his brush. All this time he had not taken his eyes from his work.

She thought, "I will pass on; perhaps I have disturbed his work."

"Oh, no, you are not disturbing me in the least; stay, if you care to do so," he said.

She had been so absorbed, his first words did not startle her, for after all, it might have been a coincidence. But this was a direct answer to her thought.

"How can you do this?" she asked looking at him wonderingly.

"How can we do anything?" he replied. "Answer me this and my first question, and I will tell you all things in heaven and earth." Still he had not looked up.

"You puzzle me," she said.

"Then do not be puzzled about anything. Be puzzled about everything. Paradoxical? Well, I believe in paradoxes, don't you?" he asked.

"I do not know," she answered.

"Well, then you should," he said. "You should know all things."

"You are modest in your requirements of me," she replied with a smile. She no longer felt ill at ease with this stranger. She moved nearer, and sat at the foot of a tree. "That's right," he said. "Let us be friends. Universal brotherhood beats the twin-soul business all to pieces.

"Unless I am related to everyone, I feel mean and selfish. When I go to church, to the theatre, unless I am related not only to the players, but to everyone in the house, from the pit to the gallery, I feel niggardly, and so it is everywhere I go. Yea, I must feel related to all creation; nothing else is life. I love all the world, don't you?"

"Why, I am afraid I do not," said Rachel hesitatingly.

"Then you are a vagabond in this beautiful world," he said positively. "I should think you would be ashamed to look in this sunlight, and say you do not love everyone. All things are glorified to-day. I met some rough looking sailors on my tramp this morning. Through their weather-beaten faces, shone the majesty of soul, and I said: 'Peace be with ye, brothers.' Further on I saw a peasant woman, with a babe at her breast. She became a Madonna more beautiful than any Raphael painted.

"And you — you, with your soft eyes and brown hair and beautifully chiseled face, are a miserable beggar—are you?" he continued.

"Alas!" she sighed, "a miserable beggar! But how should you know if my hair be light or dark? You have not looked at me."

"I can tell you more than that. You are tall and rather stately in your bearing; graceful, both from nature and efforts to become more so.

You have beautiful hands; you are gentle, have also great strength, though few know this yet. You are not vain, and you—have never loved."

Rachel had risen by this time. She had not been accustomed to having strangers talk to her in this wise.

"Just so," he replied, "but I am not a stranger. Can you not see that, feel it, or know it in some way?"

"I have not seen you before," she said. "Further than that I do not know."

"And do not wish to," he said, with a smile. "I am sorry, because we will meet often."

"You will pardon me for saying you have judged aright," she said, and moved to go.

"Oh, pray do not beg my pardon for anything. I am grateful for your indifference," he said, carelessly.

"Why are you grateful for my indifference?"

"Why? Because I am a grateful dog anyway. I am thankful for everything I have in this life. I am grateful for all the blows that have been given me, and they have not been scarce. Grateful for all things, because every little thing has had its part to play. I am thankful for all the sins I ever committed—you open those soft eyes in surprise—and they have been more numerous than could be accounted to your sunny head and pure heart, but I have gratitude for them also, because they go to make up the whole sum of my life; they have been a part of it; they have been my discipline. I am glad I have sinned, for I have repented, and through that, have gained knowledge which makes me love all the world more.

"Why, Mary Magdalen became the grandest woman of all. She had overcome the passions of the world; she could no longer be tempted. When Mary Magdalen said: 'Rabboni! which is to say, Master,' she was greater than the innocent. The Christ within her had spoken; she knew and had overcome; she had purity and wisdom. No one seems to understand this. If more could comprehend it, they would take courage and go on, instead of sinking lower into the depths of shame. And yet Christ made it so plain.

"'Of him to whom much is forgiven, the same

loveth much.' Now I have shocked your sweet, gentle soul, and should beg your pardon, but I never ask anyone's pardon. I forgive some one else for something he has done to me."

Rachel started away.

He said: "You are seeking Truth."

She stopped.

"Truth," he said, "Truth is everywhere. It appears to me there is a bit of truth in all things. The thief shows some truth—the murderer also. In my opinion the truth illustrated by the thief on the cross has never been fully understood as Christ intended. Mark me, I did not say manifested the truth, but illustrated it.

"Yes, I am glad I have sinned"—again he moved a few steps from his picture and continued: "just as I am glad I made the mistake in that shadow; it was too dark and it taught me something about white sunlight. Ah, do not all our mistakes, if understood, teach us something of the White Sunlight? Courage, sinners! Lift your heads into the Light. Added to a great sin, sorrow or love, must be the earnest, unselfish effort to help our fellow-man. This brings greatness. You have never known either, else you would not be seeking Truth in the tame way in which you do; but greatness is there. If you had loved, you would be more in earnest, and would find Truth sooner.

"I believe Christ had been all things, knew all things, else how could He have forgiven, how could He have sympathized with us as He did?"

"Re-incarnátion? Do you believe in that?" asked Rachel, showing more interest than she had done before.

"Why speak of incarnation?" the artist replied. "We are being re-incarnated every day. I am glad I was bad yesterday, because I can improve to-day. I am rejoiced I can look every fellow-creature square in the face, no matter how debased he is, clasp him by the hand and say: 'Yes, I know all about it, my brother; come on and let me help you.' I am glad I can look at the criminal with the rope around his neck and say honestly: 'I understand. We all rise from like conditions.'

"I should like to be able to sink to hell to-day,

and do a deed to-morrow the angels would smile on."

"Would you not be greater," said Rachel, "if you had all the heights and depths of life, but lived only in the heights and looked down serenely on the depths, and with compassion for others, and said: 'I could go there and come back, but — I will not?'"

"I knew you were going to say that," he replied. "The thought came to you then; it was an inspiration. The angels brought it. Every beautiful thought is an angel visit.

"But you will observe by recalling a moment, that I said: 'I should like to be able to sink to the depths and rise to the heights and be great still.' I did not say I would do it, but," and he smiled as he said it, "I think I should. To go back — it is a great thing to be in sympathy with all humanity. In truth, I believe it the greatest of all things. And the day is not distant when you will have sympathy. It may come through great suffering, I do not see clearly; but you will be redeemed through a miracle, I know not what it may be."

"The days of miracles are past," Rachel replied softly. "I hope for no such redemption. I must work out my own salvation and I do not know how."

"You are almost an angel, and yet you have not come into the realization of this through helping another. You can never become great save through this. There is many a one with a less guiltless soul, doing more good in the world than you are. 'Wisdom cries out in the streets and no man regards it.' You have been a study to me ever since I knew the circle of our lives were to touch each other. I see why you are so good, and yet there is no goodness in you; so great, and still no greatness manifesting itself. Do not think I am beginning to see this to-day. I saw it months ago. Yes, the veil is being lifted, and this shadow will vanish," he said, as he dipped his brush into the paint, and gave a touch that proved satisfactory, as he looked critically at the picture. All this time he was diligently at work, never taking his eyes from the canvas.

He gave a vigorous stroke of the brush, while his arm moved in a graceful line. "But the day of miracles is not yet over. Everything is a miracle to me to-day—that sky and sea, the cliff yonder, this hand, your angel face," he said softly, while he gave delicate touches to the clouds on his picture, "and I am waiting to see you redeemed."

"I, too, am waiting," said Rachel, as she rose and stood looking at the sea.

"Stay a moment, I will have finished soon. After all, I should like to look in your face, although I know what I shall see, but you do not know what is in mine. I never stop my work, no matter who enters my studio, and this world is mine to-day. I think this is true courtesy. If I do not allow myself to be interrupted, my friend knows he is not intruding. If I have nothing to say to him, I do not tell him a lie by saying something; but I listen to all he speaks. I hate the lies that are being told every day, by honest people. The only society in which I have sincere enjoyment is where we are truthful and I have just one honest friend. I go to that home, sometimes walk in without addressing anyone, fling myself on a sofa, stay there an hour, leave as I have come— no one has spoken and no one has lied. I love truth in all things." He gave a final stroke of the brush, put the palette on the camp-stool, walked toward Rachel and held out his hand.

She took it and looked full in his face. She saw large gray eyes—no, not that color. Well, they looked so then; to-morrow they might be something else—a face that was somewhat square and boyish. His blue-black hair was bushy, and he had a way of making himself appear almost anything by a slight movement of abruptly pulling the locks gown, or gently pushing them back from his brow—anything from a demon to a saint. A light mustache, not at all in keeping with his bushy hair, perhaps it was kind nature revealing a mouth that smiled with all the sweetness of a woman. He was slight and in stature small, though one never thought of this, there was so great a soul looking out from his eyes. He had so much greatness in his being, he made everyone else feel great.

As he held Rachel's hand, he looked deeply into her eyes, smiled, released her hand, saying "Rachel." He turned from her, took his picture from the easel, put his materials in order, and left her.

CHAPTER TWENTY-THIRD.

> Why man, he doth bestride the narrow world
> Like a Colossus; and we petty men
> Walk under his huge legs, and peep about
> To find ourselves dishonorable graves."
> — Shakespeare.

It was announced that Mazaro would give a festival. Festival of the Universe, he called it — every nation was to be represented. "Some day," he laughed, "I shall have inhabitants from the planets. There are said to be signs in the heavens now."

To Zulano, was assigned the reception of the Orientals, Mazaro desiring to see Garangula among them.

The Oriental salon looked as though borrowed from eastern skies and sunsets. Vases, holding stately palms, stood in the corners;

lamps of rare workmanship flung out many-hued flames; faint perfumes floated on the air, mingling with incense. A varying light of green and gold, flashed mysteriously, wavered a moment, then vanished. On low seats and rugs placed here and there, the guests reclined.

They moved — it was poetry. They spoke — soft music filled the room. Their wonderful jewels flashed with the varying lights. Zulona seemed a breath wafted from the Orient.... More — she was a living, breathing incarnation of their poetry. Her robe was a marvel — a strange combination of Nile green, with gold net-work over it. The net-work was woven into the texture of the silk in some places — then a space in relief, and you looked through it to the green. It was like a web in the sun. Through these golden webs at the waist, the head of a curious snake glistened. Its eyes were of the same color as the strange lights of gold and green, and when they flashed, the snake seemed to move. It looked an emblem of some lost Order. Her beautiful bosom bare, save the gold net-work caught up with small emerald beads. In the centre of the salon, was an ancient musical instrument, with dragon heads; over it hung a pale gold cloth, heavily embroidered with characters from the Koran. Leaning against the instrument, was Garangula. He had arrayed himself in his most barbaric costume—no one knew why. His bronze body was bare to the waist, save a covering of Indian ornaments; on his arm, he wore a broad band of wrought gold. In his ears were huge gold rings, set with precious stones. His hair was parted in the centre of the brow and fell in straight lines to the shoulder. From his eyes there came the same soft expression of the Oriental....yet deeper, more profound.

Rugged, massive, grand, he stood there, supreme in the consciousness of being a child of the Great Spirit. Being to him was no mystery....It was simple and profound—therefore he loved all that Was. The white man he could not understand, but he bore him no malice. He loved everything that breathed....and to him all things breathed. "The stars, the skies, the trees, the rocks, thou and Garangula belong to each other," he said, in the old days on the plains.

"Garangula is among his kindred. They have come from the Happy Hunting-Grounds," he spoke softly.

Zulona, reclining on a divan near the instrument, dropped her fan; Garangula gracefully, humbly knelt, took it up, and slowly fanned her.

A page touched a lyre. Zulona in a low voice, sang a voluptuous song of beauty.

The gold and green lights flashed, the snake moved. Garangula's eyes became transfixed.... At last, he looked down at his own girdle, and there, hidden amid the profusion of other ornaments, he found the same snake, with the same green, glistening eyes....No pen can describe the look that came over his face. He rose and glided swiftly away. Zulona was a little startled, but continued in a languorous, musical tone, the refrain being sung by voices in the distance.

Garangula was alone in the garden, his face bearing a look of pained wonder.

She of the Holy Light appeared before him.

"O Great Spirit! O Holy Light! Garangula cannot understand," he cried.

"Garangula, leave!" she whispered.

He drew his hands across his eyes and looked upward—the Light was gone. He uttered a cry that had tones of the wild animal in pain.... a lofty soul striving to comprehend. Then, in a voice of exquisite pathos, he said brokenly in his own language:

"*Klutchman chaso copa nesika tem-as*...... O mother, come now!"

In the shadow of a palm tree was Mazaro, a curious smile playing about his mouth.

The look of sorrow on Garangula's face, and the tone of grieved wonder, were seen and heard for the last time.

CHAPTER TWENTY-FOURTH.

"The fear of man bringeth a snare."
Prov. 29. 25.

Rachel returned to Uncle Jonah's house in a different state of mind. She was thoroughly aroused, and thought deeply for the first time. Though still "stately in her bearing," she walked with bowed head.

Truth was all around her, and she had not recognized it. The artist had taught her in a few words, more than all she had learned in her way of searching, and yet how did she know he had found the light? He had not said so. Would she meet him again?

The sky and sea were gray, and the waves sighed, as Rachel again walked along the shore.

She turned from the sea and followed a path into the country, but had not gone far when she met the artist, who said, with a cynical look:

"My soul tells me nothing to-day."

"Do you never learn save what your soul teaches?" asked Rachel.

"No, how could I?"

"From outward things."

"That would not be wisdom, and it is that alone we take away with us when we leave this present stage of existence."

They had been standing the while not far from each other. He said: "Let us walk. I am the only man in the world to you at this time. Give me your best thoughts. Have you ever looked at life in this way? The people who are around me to-day, are the world to me. If I am talking to a beggar, he is the only man at that time, and I must give him the best that is within me. I am a beggar, give me your highest thoughts. Perhaps your soul can teach me something."

They walked in silence, Rachel not knowing what to say.

He resumed in the same cynical tone: "I know nothing, yet I know everything. I have no head, yet have all the head there is. I am poor, but have great wealth. Oh, confusion of paradoxes! We attain Being thro' not being. Think most when we seem not to think. Live, while we care not whether we live. Have all things and yet have nothing. Pray most when naught is asked. Our power greatest as we care not, and our love strongest when we love no one."

Rachel smiled at the vehemence with which he said all this, then looking grave she thought: "I see dimly there is truth in what he says. How much I have to learn!"

"Yes, that is true, but I don't want you to talk about it now. Did you ever get inside of anyone, and look out of his eyes, and hear through his ears, and breathe and talk through his mouth?"

"No, I never had such an extraordinary experience," replied Rachel.

"I have. It isn't always pleasant," he said, with a smile. "I have also been in a condition in which I felt if there came a storm and lightning played near me, I should fly into a million atoms, then gather myself together again."

His face grew serious. Then, as if continuing the thought, he said: "I believe electricity is the Passion of the gods."

He stood a moment communing with himself; his face gradually changed.

"I feel impish to-day."

Rachel did not smile as he acted the imp in every look and motion, till he was completely transformed.

"You would not be afraid of me if I were the devil instead of an imp," he said, coming nearer. "You see, I know you well. You never felt fear in your life, did you?"

"No," replied Rachel.

"That is the reason you are great," he said. "If, added to some of your weaknesses you had fear, you would be a very small woman, but not fearing, you are great. Fear is the greatest destroyer in this world; it causes more sorrow and sin than anything else in the whole catalogue."

He was silent a long time, then said: "Yes, it is good for me to walk by the side of a pure, white soul like yours. You are good, but you don't do anything!"

Rachel grew pale.

"So you are going to try Spiritualism?" he said.

"How should you know?" she asked.

"Again, asking me the same old question. Sometime you will know. If I were to tell you now, you would not understand."

This remark did not disturb Rachel, she was not vain.

She answered: "You seem to know of many things. Do you understand Spiritualism?"

"Yes," he replied, "but I am not in the mood to discuss anything to-day. Spiritualism, in its common acceptation, is dangerous — except to the adept, and he does not need it; he has Spiritualism in its true sense. I do not believe in materializing spirit, but in spiritualizing matter. Yes, I know what you would say — there are many arguments brought up, but know this one truth, my friend, that all true development must come from within. While you are attaining this, you help every other soul. You make it possible for all to do the same. If there be anyone in the world you would like to help, send that one thoughts from the soul."

"How can I send thoughts from the soul?" she asked.

"You will learn some day. Your white soul is near the highest truths, and your mental nature will grow wonderfully through this spiritual awakening, and you will live up to your growth."

"You have received light from many sources, yet you are discordant to-day," said Rachel.

"That's right. I have been catching 'faint glimmerings'—very faint," he smiled, "since the first day I saw the light from my mother's arms. A young chap, you see, and have been moving on ever since, falling back at times further than I had progressed, vowing never to start again. And yet, there is not a religion that I have not tried to fathom."

"You have, then, studied the Eastern religions," Rachel said.

"Went to India for that purpose," he replied.

"Do you understand Theosophy? Did it bring you peace?" she asked.

"Do I look peaceful to-day? This is a very mild exhibition of myself, yet not myself. I don't know who it is."

"Someone, perhaps, has gotten inside of you," said Rachel, with a smile, "and is looking out of your eyes. You look very unlike you did when I first saw you. But you have not told me of Theosophy. I long to know," she said, with earnestness.

"Theosophy? It has deep truths in it," the artist replied. "But truths of any religion, if lived up to, would bring peace. Mark you, I did not say Theosophy was a religion. It is my opinion that the spiritual effort underlying all religions, is the same. The false interpretations of them bring disturbance to the mind. I am as universal in my feelings as I am in my beliefs. I believe in everything, but not *all* of everything. I do not wish to attain peace in a way that is incomprehensible to the meanest man that walks the earth. Christ died for all, if

He died for anybody. You see, I am in a doubtful state to-day. I am now studying that which I believe will give the true interpretation of the Soul, but all its language has not been translated. The fountain is for everyone who is thirsty."

Saying this, he caught a limb that was drooping on the side of the road, and as he swung to and fro, smilingly said, "Have a swing?"

Rachel smiled, and, turning, walked away. But when she had reached Uncle Jonah's home, her mind was still occupied with the truths the artist suggested.

CHAPTER TWENTY-FIFTH.

"Thou, O God, didst prepare of thy goodness for the poor. The Lord giveth the word."
Psalm 48. 10.

THE gates of Hyde Park swung open that beautiful morning, inviting tired people to rest beneath its grand trees, to walk by the Serpentine till they believed themselves far away in the country.

The great metropolis—the centre of the world, is always young and always old, always gay and always grave, having a completeness that meets every mood of man.

Jakusa, having just witnessed a street fight, was moving idly along with the crowd. She was thinking of Aunt Dinah and Wanda, and wondering where they were, and if Aunt Dinah had any listeners to her ghost stories.

"Little maiden,"——

Jakusa looked up, and gave a scream of delight. "I never was so glad to see anyone," she said, dancing around Garangula. "You've saved my life. I know I should have been a corpse soon."

"Garangula is happy," he said, child-like, believing the truth of Jakusa's statement.

"When did you come here?" asked Jakusa.

"Yesterday, when the great sun was high."

"Where did you go?" she asked. "Why did you not find us?"

"Garangula went where he heard great sounds. He could not understand, but he listened. Such glory burst forth that Garangula dared not move...... He saw cattle on the hills. The sun was going down.... A prairie caught fire....he heard the scream of the panthers. He saw the Happy Hunting-Grounds of his fathers....The Great Spirit was there....Garangula heard his mother's voice—it is echoing still."

His voice rose and fell in slow, measured

accents, with a music akin to the winds and seas. He seemed related to all ...yet stood alone in his native grandeur. His head was thrown back....he was listening to the echoes.

"Oh! it must have been that great man playing at St. James' Hall," cried Jakusa. "I followed the crowd in there the other day to see what was going on. I heard devils and angels' and saw all the poor people with good dinners and every body happy—that's music. When did you leave the hills where we stayed? Tell me about it, and let us sit under this tree."

"Garangula left the hills soon after the maiden went away."

"And did the English lord go with you?"

"Garangula went alone."

It was not easy to ask questions of Garangula. Jakusa wished he would be more communicative that she might be less rude—vain wish. After a few moments' silence she asked: "What made you go away?"

"Garangula wished to see the pale-face."

"What pale-face can he mean," thought Jakusa, "Rachel or Zulona?"

"Oh, the 'beautiful pale-face'," she said, diplomatically.

"The Star-Eyed-One," answered Garangula.

Awhile Jakusa sat in deep thought, then said timidly: "I dreamed of you last night."

"Didst thou? Dreams are strange things. Garangula believes in them."

Jakusa was discouraged.

"Yes, I did—it was a curious dream!"

No answer.

"Should you like to know what I dreamed?"

"If the little maiden wish to tell Garangula."

"Why, I dreamed—I dreamed I met you somewhere, and you told me why you went to see the star-eyed lady, and how—and all about it—" She suddenly stopped. There was something about Garangula that made it impossible for her to continue.

"Garangula wonders that he told all this in a dream to the little maiden. He does not know himself. He knows why he went—he wished to see the pale-face," he said, in the simplest manner.

This was little comfort to Jakusa. After a while she looked up at him. "But——"

"The maiden was going to ask how Garangula knew to find the beautiful pale-face?"

Jakusa hung her head and put her hands on her lips.

"Garangula does not know more than he knows how he went where the sounds were. The day Garangula sat alone in the wigwam he said he would find the pale-face. He went toward the rising sun without knowing why. When he reached a great village, he knew he must cross the big waters. Then the Indian went over plains and hills and through forests, on and on till he came to a great dwelling-place."

Jakusa showed no surprise; she was accustomed to mystery; still there was an interest about this she could not explain; but Jakusa never exercised her brain long at a time over anything. Soon she arose, and said: "Let us go and look at the riding." That would please him more than anything else, she thought. Garangula was dressed according to her most approved idea of an Indian. He had feathers of varied hues strung together, that hung down to his waist, and he wore many strings of beads about his neck and arms. Instead of the soft laced Indian shoe, he had on the moccasin, and walked with that gliding motion belonging to his mother. The buffalo robe added to the dignity and majesty of his bearing.

On their way to Rotten Row, they stopped at the Albert Memorial. As they walked away, he said: "Garangula does not understand."

While watching the carriages and riders dash by, he said thoughtfully: "Garangula wonders why they are all dressed in black."

"Oh," and Jakusa hesitated a moment, "Oh, I think they are in mourning for some Prince, I don't quite remember which one, but I think that is it."

"Why do they mourn for the Prince?" asked Garangula.

"Because he is dead," replied Jakusa.

"Why do they mourn for him because he is dead?"

"Oh, Garangula, I don't know. I guess it's a custom to mourn for Princes."

Garangula still wondered why they should mourn for the dead Prince. Had he not gone to the white man's Hunting-Grounds? After a while, he spoke his thoughts: "Perhaps they are not in pain, only grieving for the dead Prince."

"What can you mean?" asked Jakusa.

"Garangula was thinking from the way they all bend over, they might be in pain," he said, with such a quiet look on his face, that Jakusa broke into peals of laughter. She then took him by the hand and said: "Do let us get away; if this is the way you are going to 'do London', I'm sure you'll be the death of me."

Garangula could not comprehend what she meant. He was perfectly serious in what he had said, and when Jakusa continued to laugh, he thought it a little strange. But he had in him the basis of good breeding, that of being undisturbed under all circumstances. In truth, he never seemed to think about himself; nor did he ever laugh; he smiled, and then his face was wonderful in expression. All life to him was serious, yet he never grieved, not even when his mother went on "that long journey". The only restlessness he had ever manifested, was when he went to Tehuacana Hills and found the wigwams empty. He did not try to analyze that feeling—indeed he could not have done so. He was so nearly a normal character that it was difficult to believe he belonged to this age; and it was strange to see him in London, looking as unconscious as if he were carrying a bow and arrow on the plains.

Jakusa enjoyed to her heart's content, the sensation he created in Hyde Park that morning, but he did not know any one looked at him. He bore himself so royally and unconsciously that even the street boys did not jeer at his dress, but looked on in admiration.

As they were leaving the Park, Jakusa became very much excited; she saw a mounted policeman coming, followed by soldiers.

"Oh, Garangula, I do believe the Queen is coming! Isn't this grand?"

The guard dashed on, the royal equipage came in sight.

"That's the Queen—the one on this side!" exclaimed Jakusa.

Garangula looked at the Queen very earnestly, talking softly in the Indian language.

The pageant passed on. Jakusa and Garangula went their way through the gates. On either side was sitting a woman asking alms. The Indian looked at them and asked who they were.

"They are beggars," answered Jakusa, and explained to him how they lived.

"This day," he said, "This day is the first Garangula, the Indian, has seen a Queen and a—beggar."

CHAPTER TWENTY-SIXTH.

"Inasmuch as ye have done it unto the least of these, ye have done it unto me."
Matthew 25, Verse 31.

As they walked on, Jakusa told him where the poor lived; saying that she went down the narrow back streets, and stayed with the children, and helped them in any way she could.

"It is rough in many places, but I don't mind that; in fact, I rather enjoy it. I feel as if I belonged to them in some way; I don't think I could have lived here, if I had not found so many poor children. This place looks always the same. I guess it has been that way ever since it was built up after the flood. Don't you think so, Garangula?"

"Garangula never heard of the flood. He has

been thinking of the beggars, and wishes the little maiden would let him go with her."

Jakusa hesitated a moment; she was afraid to take him in that dress. Her generosity, however, overcame her fear, and she said: "Yes, Garangula, go. I know you will help me."

They did not walk as far from Hyde Park Corner, as one would think. It did not take long to get to the dingy, narrow streets back of Westminster—to the barren, desolate homes where "poverty is the house-holder". Not much time from the gay round of pleasure would be required to reach them. And to those who do, the memory will rise in the woods, on the sea-shore, and turn every ray of glad sunshine into blackness; every song of the birds into the wail of a starving child; change the moan of the sea over which they sigh sentimentally, into the bitter cries of famished men and women.

There are scenes in London that would make a Fiji Islander blush with shame and burn with indignation. There are chambers of living horrors, compared with which, the crimes of centuries gone by are pardonable faults of barbaric ages.

It is wonderful that in the midst of such wretchedness a city can sleep. It is strange its dreams are not peopled with images of gaunt, starving faces glaring out amid the darkness.

When returning late in the afternoon, Garangula's face had a confused look. At length, he said: "Little maiden, do the beggars belong to the same tribe as the others?"

Without waiting for a reply he continued: "Garangula, the Indian, wonders much at what he saw. He feels sorry, and believes as his mother taught him, that it is because the palefaces read books."

They came face to face with the woman whom Jakusa called "the good angel" and Garangula named: "She of the Holy Light."

She said: "The Great Spirit has led thee, and will abide with Garangula!"

The Indian answered: "O Woman of the Holy Light! Thou dost make the way bright to Garangula. He will now meet the English lord!"

CHAPTER TWENTY-SEVENTH.

*"O thou invisible spirit of wine! if thou hast no
name to be known by, let us call thee devil."*
Shakespeare.

THE autumn in London had been delightful.
The winter opened with its usual accompaniment—the fog; the sun, struggling feebly,
threw a yellowish light over all.

Garangula and Jakusa spent many hours
together seeing London, albeit the latter began
to feel that the instruction Garangula required,
taxed her rather heavily, he knew so much and
yet so little. The simple things that she
had always known, must be explained to him.
He would stand for hours in front of shop
windows, taking note of everything. Above
all, he liked to linger near the Japanese and

Indian shops. One day on Oxford Street, Jakusa asked with an amused look: "Do you know what kind of a store this is?"

"No, Garangula never looks at names. Why should he? When Garangula is alone he goes wherever he wishes without any care or thought, and he sees much beauty."

"Do you never inquire for places when you are out alone?" asked Jakusa, who was more interested in this than beauty.

"Garangula would feel strange to ask. He would think the Great Spirit was not with him."

"Do you believe the Great Spirit directs you, everywhere you go, and in everything you do?"

"Garangula believes that. Every day he says: 'O Great Spirit, speak to Garangula'."

"Are your prayers no longer than that?" asked Jakusa.

"Garangula knows not what else to say. That was all his mother taught him," he replied.

The morning had been trying to Jakusa, she could not tell why—she was cross without any special reason. When the Indian said: "Little maiden, Garangula spells the name 'Co' and 'bank', then l-i-m-i-t-e-d — what does that mean?"

Jakusa answered impatiently: "Oh, I don't know; everything in this country is limited except poverty and babies."

Garangula, not noticing her impatience, continued his questions.

"What is the matter with that man?" he asked, looking at one staggering on the sidewalk.

"He is on a bender, I guess," replied Jakusa, her momentary impatience forgotten.

"What does the little maiden mean by 'being on a bender'?"

"Well then, in polite speech, he is intoxicated — 'drunk'."

"What is 'drunk'?"

"Can't you see, Garangula, what being 'drunk' is?"

"What made him that way?"

"Drinking whisky, or beer, or ale, or wine, or something of the kind."

"What is that, little maiden?"

"'Damned fermentation', I heard a man call

it one day," replied Jakusa. "That's as good a name as any, I reckon."

"Garangula remembers his mother telling him about the white man giving her people fire-water. And this is what it was. Little maiden, why does the white man drink fire-water?"

"Oh, Lord, I don't know," answered Jakusa, very cross. "Please don't ask me any more questions to-day, Garangula."

Garangula was silent for a moment.

"Will the little maiden let Garangula ask one more question?" he said, in that musical voice of his, no one could resist.

Jakusa looked at him and smiled. "Yes, just 'one more'."

"Does the white man enjoy 'being drunk'?" Jakusa laughed.

"See, Garangula," her tone changing; "it is growing dark; I noticed when we started out the sun looked 'queer', that is what they say here when they are ill, and the sun looked sickly this morning—I guess that is the proper word to use. I suppose he has grown worse and retired; leastwise he hid himself from view long ago, and it grows darker.

"Oh, Garangula, I do believe there is going to be one of those black fogs in which folks get lost and never find their way."

"How could one get lost?"

"It would be very easy for me, so I am not going to risk it," said Jakusa excitedly, and motioning violently to a cabman, left Garangula, who could not be persuaded to go with her.

Through the black fog, mid all the confusion ....then the silence—the Indian walked on quietly, his figure dimly outlined by the faint yellow light of the lamps.

CHAPTER TWENTY-EIGHTH.

"The sorrows of hell compassed me about."
Samuel, 22. 6.

.

It was more than a week before Rachel saw the artist. The old spirit of unrest was upon her. She walked toward the sea—the clouds hung low, the waves sighed as they beat the cliffs; the whole world moaned.

As she neared the cliff, she heard—"To-morrow and to-morrow" in the same voice and yet its tone so changed, she scarcely recognized it; she stopped undecided whether to go further—the voice repelled her.

"I am your brother," he said; "speak to me."

She went forward, but could not see him; going behind the cliff she found him crouched underneath the ledge — a torn canvas on an easel, was lying in front of him. His large eyes that had looked at her so kindly, were now protruding from a face that looked like distorted humanity. His attitude was like a prisoner in his cell; he seemed an old man.

"The first day you saw me," his voice not changing its gutteral tone, "I loved all things, believed and had faith in all, but now——

"Yesterday," and his voice changed to wonderful sweetness, "ah! yesterday was beautiful. I was helping an old farmer make hay. I had heavenly thoughts. I worked until I was very tired, and quiet and peaceful. As I drew the scythe through the grass, the blade glistened in the sun, and in the sunbeams above, a Madonna floated—a Madonna the angels hover around. Could I paint such a one, all men would look upon it and realize motherhood as ne'er before. And," his tone musical as a song, "and with that Madonna your image was blended—it was your face, your eyes, and the whole was divine. I looked up each time I swung the blade through the grass. I could have worshipped you yesterday. To-day I loathe the very sight of you.

"I loathe everybody in the universe—everything and everyone, and of all things, myself the most. I am concentrated with a double compound of nausea."

Rachel smiled in spite of herself.

"There is nothing in all the world but selfishness," his voice now sounding like the growl of a dog. "The word stares at me wherever I turn. The landscape that was holy to me yesterday, is desecrated to-day.

"Selfishness, selfishness. It is selfish to love or to hate; selfish to joy and to sorrow; to have friends or to have enemies; to work or to be idle. And aspiration, bah! it is robed in a damnable cloak of selfishness. The very name turns me sick. The body is selfish, and I fail to see why the soul is not—it is. I am so filled with loathing and hate, my whole being is reeking in it. I hate vice; I hate virtue. I hate death, and life more than death, if there be any degrees in hate, and I suppose there are degrees in everything, and yet the whole world and all things in it, are reduced to one common level to me to-day. I hate light, and darkness, and sea, sky and earth—all things are coated over—ugh! there is nothing—and yet, oh God, I wish there were nothing—it would be better than this!

"No, do not try to comfort me. 'Miserable comforters are ye all'."

Rachel smiled, drew her cloak about her and sat down near him.

He looked at her from under his eyebrows. Though ungrateful, it relieved him to pour out his feelings.

"Oh, God! I cannot tell you the unrelieved confusion I have been in since last evening."

Rachel, who was naturally sensitive to tones of the voice, gave an expression indicative of her nerves being put to severe test.

"Yes," he said, "I know this grates on your soul in every way, and I don't care. You are disgusted, but I am sodden in disgust and despair. I am clothed in fears and sullen dejections of heart and striving. There will be nothing left of me but a nervous skeleton with sandwich chest and weak knees, and a countenance of idiotic apathy."

With that he laughed sardonically, and crouched lower behind the rock, his head bowed on his knees.

Rachel turned from him.

"Listen!" he continued, "the waves cry out. And my heart wails in unison—unclean beasts are in the holy temple! Oh, it is so cold! I weep salt-brine tears. I have shrieked with agony of desolation. Yes, there is eternal hell as well as eternal heaven, and 'hell and destruction are never full'. Now is eternity, and we can plunge without limit, deeper, deeper into the night of Nothing. I feel that God's face is to be hidden from me. Oh, this terrible isolation! I have not had peace for so long, so long. The temporary calms have been merely stupors, unintelligent pauses, to awake again to frights, panics alternated by devilish furies and blasphemings. Rachel, I shall be cursing you presently. Shriekings, moans, and blasphemies dry on my tongue, making it foul, and my bones to ache, and my teeth rotten. The material asserts its hideous supremacy. Oh, that I could be given to Myself! I am loosed from my anchorage and get tossed in miasma and whirlpools of all surrounding mortal thoughts! The story of error is unfathomable!"

Rachel arose and passed from their retreat.

She walked on through the wind and rain; as she reached the door of her home, she was repeating his words in a bewildered way.

CHAPTER TWENTY-NINTH.

> "Nay, do not think I flatter;
> For what advancement may I hope from thee,
> That no reverence hast but thy good spirits
> To feed and clothe thee?
>   *   *   *
> "Give me that man
> That is not passion's slave, and I will wear him
> In my heart's core,—ay, in my heart of hearts,
> As I do thee."
> Shakespeare.

IT was the Golden Carnival. The aristocrats of British society were gathered together. Noble women presided over the brilliant scene, and served in the decorated booths, containing articles of rare workmanship, vases, flowers, and a thousand beautiful things to be sold for the benefit of the poor.

In one of the booths, crowded with duchesses and princesses, stood a form straight as an arrow, a crown of eagle feathers on his head. A tall young Englishman, who had just entered, sprang forward and cried: "Garangula! By Jove! I'm glad." And he shook Garangula's hand again and again, with the cordial grasp of a true Englishman. Garangula's face had a look of contentment and joy.

Close by a booth, more exclusive than the others, stood a man watching Garangula. A dark frown gathered on his brow, and a deep curse escaped his lips.

"I will bide my time," he said. "He shall come to me. He shall come to me." He put his hand on his brow and staggered backwards, as he cried out: "Oh, handsome Garangula!" Then turning away, Mazaro spoke in the low, determined voice: "I will have the power to draw and hold him. I know how it can be attained, and it shall be mine. I will send my spirit to the very abode of the Evil One, rather than be thwarted in this. Come," he whispered, as if speaking to unseen hosts, "surround me—take me, body and soul—I care not, so you endow me with power. In the name of all the gods of light and of darkness, I demand it! Give me knowledge that I may have power. Come, power——" He sank on a seat exhausted, and covered his face with his hands.

From that night at the Golden Carnival, the world knew but little of Mazaro. He went back to the Strange Palace, and spent his days in seclusion.

"Of all the places in London to find you," continued Lord Carleton. "But then you have always been surprising me in some way."

"Garangula trusts the surprises have been happy to the English lord."

"Not always, Garangula. You see you have taught me to be sincere. I have shocked my sisters till they had to use their smelling salts. They declare I have become a perfect barbarian, and it is all your fault, Garangula."

"Garangula does not know what the English lord means."

"I am too delighted at finding you again to tell you. I arrived yesterday, and early this morning began searching for you, hoping without any reason, that you might be here. Why did you not write to me?"

"Because Garangula could not say what he wished in writing."

Lord Carleton looked at him again, and said: "You are the same, only a trifle more serious than in the old ranch days. Ah, they were good old days, Garangula. Tell me about yourself—have you seen the pale-face?"

"The Indian found the pale-face."

"Where did you find her?"

"Garangula does not know. It is far away."

A tone in Garangula's voice, made Lord Carleton change the subject. "This Carnival," he said, "is the most talked of thing going now, every paper has something about it."

"Garangula does not read papers."

"No, of course not," said Lord Carleton. "Well, then, come on, and let me enlighten you a little; you see I am delighted to resume our old relationship."

"Garangula is no less so than the English lord."

"Spoken like the Indian of old," rejoined Lord

Carleton, as he linked Garangula's arm in his. "If you say such things to the beautiful paleface, I should think you would soon win her heart," he continued carelessly.

Garangula replied without embarrassment: "Garangula said to the beautiful pale-face what he felt."

Lord Carleton was annoyed at his baffled curiosity; perhaps he would learn more, if he talked on other subjects.

"Have you examined a catalogue to know who all these charming ladies are?"

"The Indian was content to look at them," replied Garangula.

"What a sincere admirer of beauty you are. Have you seen any one here as handsome as the beautiful pale-face?"

"Yes; but not so much expression."

"My pupil has advanced. I am proud of you, but I feel jealous," replied Lord Carleton. "Has any one been reading to you?"

"The beautiful pale-face has been teaching Garangula."

"What has she been teaching you?"

"Garangula does not know."

Lord Carleton laughed in spite of his displeasure.

"Does she read to you as I did? And from what kind of books?" He was determined, now, to learn all about it.

"The beautiful pale-face did not often read to Garangula."

"What, then—talk to you?"

"Sometimes."

"What did she talk about?"

"Garangula did not know, but he thought it very beautiful."

"Don't know what she said!"

"No," Garangula answered.

"What good, then, was to be attained through her teaching?"

"Garangula does not know."

They walked on in silence. Lord Carleton thought he knew his friend. "One is never sure of anything when a woman is connected with it," he was thinking, when Garangula said: "And she made motions sometimes."

Lord Carleton stopped, looking at him in blank dismay.

"The most beautiful motions," Garangula continued.

"And what did she make beautiful motions to you for?" cried Lord Carleton, quite irritated by this time.

"Garangula does not know."

"Well, by Jove! But it is no use trying," he said, as he looked into Garangula's face.

"Let me tell you something of these celebrities. The one in the second booth from us, is Duchess of Belgravia, one of the most noted society ladies in England. Next to the Duchess, is the Hon. Miss ——, I forget her name. I have been from London so long, it will take some time to become versed in society affairs. But the lady is just out this season, and has created a great sensation, I am told; and for once, society is right—she is beautiful."

"What does the English lord mean by 'being out'?"

"Oh, this is her first season in society, don't you know?" replied Lord Carleton.

"Garangula does not know. But the lady is beautiful like jewels. She obeys the Law of Succession."

"'Obeys the Law of Succession!'" cried Lord Carleton in astonishment. "What can you mean, Garangula?"

"Garangula does not know; he cannot explain it, but he feels it," replied the Indian in nowise disconcerted.

Lord Carleton smiled, yet his face was not entirely free from solicitude.

"It makes her appear 'well bred', the English lord would say. Garangula thinks she looks like a child of the Great Spirit—one who has never wandered from the Happy Hunting-Grounds."

"While the one to her right is vulgar," answered Lord Carleton. "I begin to see what you mean."

"Garangula would say she had lost her way from the Happy Hunting-Grounds."

"Look at the last booth in this room," said Lord Carleton. "There is one of the most charitable women in all England. She spends a large income every year in helping the poor, besides she is wonderfully clever; but she is not what we call a real lady. The one opposite—well, she is not noted for anything, I believe, but for having bankrupted two husbands with her foolish extravagance; but she is a lady. The one you thought had lost her way from the Happy Hunting-Grounds is a countess. I wonder what she would say to that."

"Garangula meant no rudeness; he feels sorry."

Lord Carleton burst out laughing at the oddity of the situation. "Imagine a Texas Indian being sorry for one of the wealthiest and oldest titled families in England. This is delicious!" and he laughed again.

"Why not?" asked Garangula.

"It grows more delicious, but it is no use wasting words on you, Garangula, for with all your learning from the beautiful pale-face, there are some facts you cannot understand."

"Garangula wishes he could understand what the English lord means by a real lady," said the Indian very seriously.

"Oh, Garangula, much as I like you, I could never make you comprehend the situation, besides I would rather you would not."

Lord Carleton changed his tone and said: "I want you to love my country."

"Garangula does love the English lord's country."

"Thank you, Garangula. There is no country under the sun like old England, but I am afraid there are some things in society here that could not be viewed with your eyes, without your expressing your sympathy again."

"Garangula does not know what the English lord means. The Indian intended no unkindness," he said, humbly.

"Be assured you can never offend me as long as you remain Garangula. This Carnival," Lord Carleton continued, "is for the benefit of the poor children. The money paid for these beautiful things goes to help them."

"Then Garangula must buy something. He wishes to get it from the one who is 'just out'."

The Indian looked on the display, the flash of jewels, the elegant costumes, the noble dames, heroic looking men, and said: "It seems strange ——"

Lord Carleton smiled, but answered nothing. They had reached the booth. The Indian leaned forward and said: "Would the Lady-of-the-Sunbeam allow Garangula to have that?"—he looked at a curious bit of workmanship— "Garangula does not know what to call it."

The lady looked confused. Lord Carleton came to the rescue, and said, as he lifted his hat, "Pray pardon my friend; he is a savage. You know only barbarians are permitted to speak the truth."

Her face was a lovely crimson as she answered: "America has not taught Lord Carleton to give up compliments. Have you forgotten Elise Pendleton?" and she offered her hand cordially as an old friend.

"Ah, you girls change so," replied Lord Carleton. "When I remember how small you were five years ago, I feel quite aged."

They chatted pleasantly for a while, and when other patrons came, Lord Carleton said: "We must not intrude longer."

"Come to mamma's 'At Home' next Thursday; she will be delighted to see you," Miss Pendleton said.

"Oh, thank you," replied Lord Carleton. "May I bring my friend?" he looked at Garangula.

"Lord Carleton knows he has that privilege," she answered.

The article was given to Garangula; he looked at the lady and said: "Thou hast the manner of love."

Miss Pendleton blushed again. Lord Carleton laughingly said: "Do be as frank as you were five years ago, and say you think he is the handsomest man you ever saw."

She turned from them under the pretense of attending to some one, and they walked away, many eyes following the high-bred Englishman in his fashionable suit, and the handsome Indian in picturesque costume.

CHAPTER THIRTIETH.

> "O, but man, proud man!
> Drest in a little brief authority
> Most ignorant of what he's most assured,
> His glassy essence—like an angry ape,
> Plays such fantastic tricks before high heaven,
> As make the angels weep."
>
> Shakespeare.

GARANGULA became Lord Carleton's honored guest, and before many weeks he was the sensation of London society. He still called his host the "English lord," and could not be persuaded to say anything else. He never addressed anyone by name. Perhaps it was that which delighted the ladies; he always distinguished them in some complimentary way, and his vocabulary in this respect was inexhaustible.

"You are cultivating my appreciation," said Lord Carleton; "I had no idea the ladies possessed so many charming qualities. Every woman in the world could be either picturesque, beautiful, or interesting, but she is not."

"Garangula has never seen a woman who was not. All people are interesting to Garangula. He looks in the eyes of each one, and says: 'Thou art a child of the Great Spirit'."

Lord Carleton clasped Garangula's hand, but was silent. They left the house and taking a cab, were soon on their way. Not, however, before Lord Carleton had provided a lunch of fruits, nuts, and vegetables, saying, "Garangula, I wish you would let me order what I know you like. My mother would be happy to have me do so."

"Garangula is grateful to the English lord for remembering his simple tastes, but he would not have anything before him that was not partaken by the others," he replied, humbly.

"I could never understand, Garangula, why you do not eat meat. Your mother must have done so."

"Garangula's mother ate meat that was killed on the plains and in the forests, but his father did not. Garangula has known him to live on bread and water many weeks. Garangula loved his mother, but in many ways he is like his father."

Lord Carleton took great interest in accompanying Garangula through London, not merely because he was his guest; he enjoyed the Indian's opinion, and also wished to see the result of his teaching. He would often think what Garangula would have said five years ago. Occasionally, the influence of the beautiful paleface appeared, and never failed to irritate Lord Carleton—not that it was without merit, but he hated the source.

Lord Carleton did not tell Garangula the names of the places they visited. All were of interest to the Indian.

"I shall take him," said Lord Carleton, "to places all the world knows. I wish to see them through his eyes. It will be like visiting a new country."

It was still early morning when they reached Tower Hill. The sun was shining, throwing in relief the gray, old building. The White Tower, surrounded by its four turrets, produced a vivid impression on Garangula.

"Will the English lord tell Garangula," he said at last, "something of the interesting monument? It appears so to the Indian."

"Well said," replied Lord Carleton. "It is a memorial of eight centuries of inhumanity."

The Indian shivered.

"I would rather not explain to you," said Lord Carleton, "lest you think the white man more cruel."

"The English lord cannot mean the white man has wronged his own people?"

"Yes."

"Then Garangula wonders——" he did not finish the sentence. "Once, after Garangula's mother went on her long journey, Garangula sat thinking of the wrongs of his people; he said: 'If they were children of the Great Spirit, how could they have been killed'? Something whispered: 'They were not killed; they awoke and found themselves in the Happy Hunting-Grounds'. Garangula arose comforted. He knows it is well with the red man."

"Heaven bless you, Garangula! I believe you will convert me yet. I am sure they all awoke in the Happy Hunting-Grounds, if they were as noble as you. I wonder if the poor victims that were beheaded here, awoke and found 'they were not killed'. Here is the very spot where they were—not exactly scalped, you know," said Lord Carleton, smiling, "but their heads cut off with an ax!"

"Why? Did they own homes someone else wanted?"

"No, it was on account of their religious principles, and other reasons."

"What does the English lord mean by 'religious principles'?"

"It is what you would call belief in the Great Spirit," said Lord Carleton. "Ah, I wonder," he continued, growing thoughtful, "if it were such a day as this! The sun rising from the misty clouds, shining on the Thames, then glancing on the turrets as the bell tolls, telling the prisoners, lives must be sacrificed to-day. They kneel in their bare, desolate dungeons the last time; they are led down the winding stairs—the priest goes before—the solemn procession is coming up the Hill, the sun still shining; souls are to be set free from their earthly tenements to wend their flight—whither?"

"Garangula cannot understand all the English lord means. The terror of the cruelty comes over him. But they found themselves with the Great Spirit."

They stood silent a moment, Lord Carleton said: "I am beginning to have a little of your faith, Garangula. I am not an irreverent man; I have never thought upon the serious side of life, except the ways of the world. This day will be a memorable one to me. Let us enter the gates.

"This was first a palace for royalty," continued Lord Carleton. "After passing through many gradations, it became a prison—now, it is a curiosity the world visits.

"We will go to the White Tower, where you will see a magnificent collection of old armor, most carefully arranged—the trophies from Waterloo, and the instruments of torture that are witnesses of our refined cruelty. You see we did not give our victims a sudden death by scalping; we stood by and watched their agony."

Looking at the armor, Garangula said: "What was all this for?"

Lord Carleton could not answer at first; he thought he had grown accustomed to Garangula's simple questions, but like Jakusa, he was sometimes at a loss for words.

"For? Why, they used these to protect themselves in battle. It would be difficult for a man to be hit behind that."

Lord Carleton saw the scorn in Garangula's face, and was puzzled. "What is it, Garangula?" he hastily said.

"Garangula cannot say. He is in the English lord's country."

"Speak, my friend; I promise not to be offended."

"The English lord will forgive," he answered, "but Garangula could not help feeling sorry for the man who would protect himself behind that," and he looked at the armor. "Garangula remembers hearing his mother tell how one of her ancestors fought in the midst of battle with the white man. When the pale-faces crowded around him, he flung aside his buffalo robe, bared his breast, and cried: 'Big Indian Chief is not afraid. He can begin his long journey with his face toward the white man!'—then gave one long war-cry and fell, his face to the foe."

Garangula had unconsciously expanded his chest, thrown back his head, and his eyes flashed as he said the last words in his mother's language.

"I am reserving something beautiful for you," said Lord Carleton, as they proceeded to the room containing the Crown Jewels.

Garangula spoke no word while they looked at the wonderful jewels.

A shade of sadness stole over his face.

"What troubles you?" asked Lord Carleton.

"Garangula thought of the women who sat by the gates."

They turned away, and walked from the Tower down to the Thames, and took a boat, Garangula asking to use the oars. When they were seated, he looked back and said softly, "Garangula wonders why the white man keeps the Tower and shows it to strangers."

A picture they made as they rowed down the Thames. The aristocratic face of the blonde Englishman, turned with admiration toward the Indian, who was using the oars with graceful, broad sweeps. One's thoughts went back to Garangula, the Sachem of the Onondagas, and wondered if the Indian with Lord Carleton, were a descendant of that chieftain, of whom it was said, he "was magnanimous as well as courageous."

This red man knelt over Nature's well, parted the ferns, drank of the free water, rose, and the ferns closed again. He built his fire on the ground and cooked his simple meal, lay down trusting the Great Spirit, and slept. The next morning he went his way, leaving the winds to scatter the ashes, and the grass to spring up where they had been. Who shall say he was not more of a god than the white man? These thoughts came to Lord Carleton. After a long silence, he said: "Garangula, it has been good to bring you here to-day, yet I could wish we had not come."

"Garangula does not understand why—— Hark! Did the English lord hear a voice?"

"No, I heard nothing," replied Lord Carleton.

"A voice called to Garangula. He must listen and wait."

The dip of the oars grew fainter and fainter as they floated down the Thames....the Indian still listened.

CHAPTER THIRTY-FIRST.

> "This precious stone set in the silver sea,
> * * * * *
> This blessed spot, this earth, this realm, this England."
> —Shakespeare.

THE day after the visit to the Tower, Lord Carleton and Garangula went to Windsor Castle. When returning, Lord Carleton said curiously: "Garangula, what have you most enjoyed in London?"

"Garangula does not know the name of the place. He went through gates, on beside tall columns, feeling exalted. Through two doorways Garangula passed and found himself in a room surrounded by figures of men and women, cut out of stone and marble. Garangula had strange feelings."

"What were your feelings?" asked Lord Carleton.

"Garangula knows not; he bowed his head and said: 'The Great Spirit is kind to the Indian'."

"The British Museum," thought Lord Carleton, "and he was doubtless in the Elgin Room. I feel humiliated. I have never been there but once, and it did not occur to me that the Lord had been particularly gracious in giving me that privilege. I felt rather bored than otherwise, for I had two ladies with me, one an American, who constantly exclaimed, 'How lovely!' while the English lady chimed, 'Perfectly charming!' until I failed to recognize Venus de Milo from Diana, if they were there, which I am by no means sure."

"Then Garangula stood in the room," resumed the Indian, "where he saw figures."

"Statues," corrected Lord Carleton.

"Statues," said the Indian, "of grand looking men and women. He began taking their attitudes. He was one of them and they carried him to their country where he saw men and women walking the earth like great spirits. After a long time Garangula came back, and walked up and down the room, talking to the statues. He knows not how long he was thus, but Garangula's spirit seemed to—ah, he cannot tell—he cannot tell, he knows not what happened, it was all so strange. But Garangula will know some day," he said, confidently.

"I am glad you felt all this," said Lord Carleton. "It will make you forget prosaic London for a while at least."

"Garangula does not wish to forget London. He feels poetry here."

"I realize London is the greatest city in the world—one feels he is really living nowhere else. It is full of interest with its cathedrals, palaces, art galleries, and museums, but I, a true Englishman, fail to see its poetry."

"Garangula has nowhere felt the poetry the London fog gives," said the Indian quietly.

"The London fog!" cried Lord Carleton.

"Yes. Both the yellow and black fog, but the yellow fog most of all. Garangula will remember always, the first time he saw the yellow fog—a thousand forms came to him as he looked at the trees in the park that rose out of the yellow light, and heard birds singing softly from the branches, birds of strange plumage coming from an unknown land; dark, old buildings changed into mysterious castles, which Garangula peopled with images."

Lord Carleton listened with increasing surprise. This was the longest, unbroken sentence he had ever heard Garangula use, and his language was different; was it influenced by the teachings of the beautiful pale-face?

"The yellow cloud," continued the Indian, "hovered over all, lending a distance to all things. This, with the hush, as the fog came on, left an impression that is with him still. The black fog is not poetical, but solemn and dramatic."

"Yes, very, when one gets lost in it," replied Lord Carleton. He looked at the Indian and wished the beautiful pale-face had never appeared on the plains.

"Soon after Garangula had seen the yellow and black fogs, he went to a building where there were many rooms hung with pictures. Garangula did not look at them till he entered one, where his delight was boundless. The fog seemed to hang over the pictures. He had not known they could be so, even after all the beautiful pale-face had taught him. She told him much about pictures, but she never spoke of that which he saw there."

Lord Carleton frowned, but the Indian exclaimed: "O, these fog pictures, Garangula cannot explain! He never cared before to know who painted a picture — he said he will understand some time. Then he saw a word — Turner. Garangula thinks that was the name of the man who painted them. Garangula will meet him in the Happy Hunting-Grounds."

"I do not doubt it," replied Lord Carleton.

The Indian could not have a better companion than Lord Carleton. He honestly admired his childlike simplicity and faith, and showed to Garangula the best side of his own character. Garangula was impressionable, yet unchangeable; his accent was almost the same as Lord Carleton's, and many phrases had taken coloring from the pale-face, but nothing could change the ideal humanity in that half Indian, who had combined in him the simple faith of his savage mother with the influence of the deep learning of his father.

"Save once, Garangula has seen nothing so poetical as the yellow London fog," he continued, earnestly.

"What was that?" asked Lord Carleton.

"After the Indian's mother went on the long journey, her child wandered from the hills, far away among the snows. One night, Garangula, wrapped in a buffalo robe, lay on the ground, but he slept not. There had been a snow over which sleet and rain had fallen, the trees were covered with ice. The Lamp of the Great Spirit burned in the sky to show this scene to His children. The earth seemed of crystal. Garangula imagined there were crystal caves underneath the white bushes and trees in the distance, and a frozen river curved in and out among the rocks, and strange beings lived there; they were robed in white, wearing jewels made of white stones. They played on harps and sang. He heard the echoes among the trees that moved, and wondered if the Lamp hung in their sky, and the white-robed people could find their way to the Happy Hunting-Grounds.

"It was real to Garangula then. It is poetry now. The fog was poetry when he first saw it, and is poetry still. Garangula knows not why."

Lord Carleton looked at him wonderingly. "Was the Indian changing after all? Would culture rob him of his wild nature?" But Garangula looked the same, while he said: "Garangula thinks poetry is the only real thing. It speaks of the Happy Hunting-Grounds."

"I shall enjoy taking him to Westminster Abbey," thought Lord Carleton. "I hope he has not been there. Curiously enough, while I told him of many things in the world, I said little of the interesting places in London. I wonder if he has been drawn in that mysterious way, to any religious service? He had never heard a sermon when he left me."

"Have you been to any of the cathedrals — churches?" asked Lord Carleton. "But why ask? I am afraid I have neglected your education very sadly after all. Have you been in a place where the people rose and sung, then listened to a man speak?"

"One day," he answered, "Garangula was walking, and heard deep-toned music. He went in the dwelling-place whence it came, and the people stood, and sang together. Garangula listened with joy. When the song was finished, some sat down, leaning forward, others knelt. Then a man spoke loud to someone afar off. Garangula thought this very strange, but he did not look up, as everyone else had bowed head. The man continued to speak, and so bewildered Garangula that he knew not what to do. He said: 'O Thou most high God! Who sittest upon Thy throne in the heavens, draw nigh unto us poor, miserable sinners'.

"Garangula began to feel anxious. The one to whom the man spoke, seemed to be far away from all people, and he begged him to come down and help trample the devil underfoot, 'for the enemy is around us', he cried, 'the enemy encompasseth us about; we are sore afraid that we will be overcome by temptation. O, Lord, spare us from the burning lake of fire and brimstone——!'

"Garangula could listen no longer. He grew afraid, because he did not know who was coming to the people in that house. He feared something terrible would rush upon them and destroy them. The man had said, 'Thou alone can rescue us', and the one to whom he called, still seemed far away. Garangula was afraid all would be destroyed before he could get there. It was the first time that Garangula knew fear. He trembled and felt something awful, terrible would swallow him. If he had known what the awful thing was, he would have been courageous and fought with it, but he did not understand. He looked around quietly, but saw nothing, and thought perhaps the ground would move and let all the people down into that burning lake. Garangula pictured himself breathing the scorching flames and crying out. He forgot about the Happy Hunting-Grounds. The clear streams, green banks, and beautiful hills all drifted away. The terror of that burning lake separated him forever from them, and he thought he would never find them again.

"Such a terror seized Garangula that he could endure it no longer. He bowed his head lower and lower through great respect for these people who were braver than he, and fled noiselessly. He ran on and on, till he came to great trees. He looked up at the sky, so peaceful. He touched the tree 'neath which he stood, the branches reaching out to care for him. Garangula stretched forth his arms to the sun, the sky, and ground, and cried: 'O loving mother, receive him who has lost his way! Help Garangula who is far away from the Happy Hunting-Grounds. He is afraid!' Then Garangula knelt on the ground, crying out again and again: 'O Great Spirit, help Thy lost child!'

"Leaves came down and kissed Garangula's upheld hands and face. He closed his eyes and knelt lower to the earth till prostrate on the ground, his face resting against the trunk of the tree. A great peace stole over him. He heard soft music. Garangula does not know how long he stayed there. When he opened his eyes, the Lamp of the Great Spirit was lighted in the heavens. Garangula arose, went his way, and was not afraid."

Lord Carleton turned his face from the Indian as he ceased speaking; his eyes were moist.

CHAPTER THIRTY-SECOND.

> "Eye hath not seen, nor ear heard, neither have entered into the heart of man, the things which God hath prepared for them that love him."
>
> 1, Cor. 2, 9.

RACHEL stood at the gate looking down the country road—a vague hope had come that something might happen to help her restless spirit. The hope grew stronger—some one was coming—coming gently as the twilight, and Rachel ran to meet Jakusa's "good angel"—the woman whose name was Namora, meaning Light.

"How could you know I longed for you?" and Rachel lifted her hands toward her. Namora looked long and earnestly in the soft, brown eyes, and they went on together.

Rachel thought she had never seen Namora

look so youthful. After partaking a light meal, she conducted her to the little room that looked inviting with its bare, spotless floor and white curtains. They sat by the window through which the moonlight fell; after a long silence Namora said, in exquisitely tender tones:

"This is an anniversary with me."

Rachel felt a moment's surprise. She had never associated anniversaries of any kind with Namora.

"Yet time is not." The voice was still sweet, but stronger. "Now is eternity. I will tell you a story. Should you like to hear?"

Rachel answered her without words.

"Ages ago," Namora said, "a Russian girl of noble birth loved a Chaldean, imbued with deep, religious feeling. Being in humble life, her hand was denied him, and they were separated." Namora's voice sank into a musical monotone, and her face expressed perfect love and peace— "I was the girl who loved the Chaldean."

"Impossible!" said Rachel, "and yet, I have wondered how one so young, possessed such power."

"You will understand," replied Namora, "and through knowledge, discover the Fountain of Youth. Soon after our parting," Namora resumed, "I felt that my loved one was in great danger. Then, that his spirit had fled. In my agony, I cried, 'Let me go!' and fell forward unconscious, my body apparently lifeless, my spirit joined his. We met the same as when we parted. For many days I lay in that trance-like state, and my spirit wandered with his in the land called Mystery. Among many wonderful things, those which impressed me, were the ruins of a great city under the ground.

"The most interesting of these, were two palaces in perfect preservation. Pink and black marble they were, and strange they looked amid the ruins of thousands of years. The blending of color in the Pink Palace, was the effect of the rainbow seen from the mountain top. A mist ever hovered about the colonnades, in the recesses, whose only shadows were a deeper pink. The floor inlaid with mosaics of precious stones — pink, amber, gold, and green intermingling with the rising mist, gave one the sensation of walking on sunbeams in space. One became a part of the mist, the colors, and the incense, and tried to gather the incense close, but the mist and colors came with it. A sweet, subtile perfume floated also, and beckoned to deeper colors and more shadowy mists, where the incense was not. Soft music was there, faintly voluptuous, that grew stronger with the perfumes and colors. Beings wondrous fair floated above all, and with every motion of their perfect limbs, the colors and music gathered closer and closer, till one closed his eyes and almost ceased to breathe.

"My brain wavered.... My mind made a feeble effort to grasp a far-off memory.... As the wondrous forms moved, all the air grew tremulous and the shadows darker. I, though formless, saw my own form standing among them, and from me the incense had floated far away.... By and by, appeared a woman fairer than the most fair. She beckoned us to a Sacred Altar. The sight at first, was so dazzling, our eyes were blinded.... We saw the seven colors radiating from the centre of the

Altar. Side by side each ray of color, was a note in music. A radiant being appeared, bearing on her brow, in letters of gold, the word—Art. One saw the sunset, the rainbow, the colors of the sea, and all things beauteous....Every tone was heard from the soft song to the music of the spheres.

"The colors and sounds grew more dazzling, more intricate, and higher harmonies were heard....Another appeared. On her brow was written—Poetry. The colors and sounds radiated again....They waved in light....The mystic meaning of Form was shadowed forth.

"My love and I went on together. We came to the Black Palace. From wondrous light and warmth and color, we passed to gloom. All things were shadowy, mystic—symbolical. On the walls, hieroglyphics dimly lighted, were found. The floor was paved with black and purple stones. In dark corners, sphinxes sat in solemn grandeur. Mystic books were hidden under the east corner of the Palace. The most wonderful of these, was one which contained the characters of the Zodiac. There were maps carved on a bituminous substance, giving the history of men's lives thousands of years ago. We found there an image carved in the same substance and inlaid with gold. It was the face of a Chaldean—the one who instructed me in the hieroglyphics of the heavens. I have gone back to remote periods when men were deep in darkness. My present life is my own choice. I am what I have made myself. Thought is a power that turns the scales of what man calls Destiny. Man rules his own destiny. Ay, he originates it.

"I will tell you more of the Black Palace. Through a square doorway, on either side of which were simple massive columns, we entered a hall of solid masonry with smooth black walls, and found ourselves in the Whispering Gallery of Thought. Each one gathered those of his own past and their attraction.... To some, this hall became a church and they stood before sacred altars. To others, it was transformed into a thoughtless world where men and women lived in the senses only. Some were radiantly happy, drawing the holiest influences. Many were plunged into deepest hell, and writhed in the most horrible torture, breathing forth curses. Some shouted aloud for joy, and cried: 'Most Holy!' These were the ones who had helped the poor and suffering.

"We went on and on. The veiled figure of Isis stood by a sarcophagus in a dark corner. We drew near, and looked on our own forms through eons and eons of time. A strange feeling seized me.... My eyes opened to the brilliant life we led in the Pink Marble Palace.... Our term of probation in the Black Palace where my love and I were prepared for the journey....

"With this, there came great memories. I could remember that life distinctly, but from the moment we left our bodies, all was blank to my present embodiment. I could not then understand....

"After a time, I know not how long, a wave, like the rushing of mighty waters, swept over us. We stood in a Temple ... The gods were assembled and counseled together. They spoke of Celestial Love—Transmuted Force, the Sacred Fire that burned with power and splendor, but did not consume. It gave to man the power of the gods, and enabled him to stand upon the Great Mount.

"Then we were Initiated.

"I bore a Flaming Torch above my head. He knelt and kissed my robe.

"The Flaming Torch burst forth enveloping us, then circled into Light. A voice said: 'Light is greater than Fire'."

Rachel's eyes were riveted on Namora's face, while she was speaking. But suddenly a strange drowsiness overcame her. The eyelids drooped for a moment, when they opened, the waning of a radiant light was perceptible to Rachel's senses — Namora was gone ——!

CHAPTER THIRTY-THIRD.

> "Watchman, what of the night?"
> Isaiah, 21. 11.

Rachel had entered the depths. Until man begins the search for Truth he is wonderfully tame, then he becomes godlike in his very doubt. As the tumult rages he sometimes bows before the storm, but never gives up the struggle.

"Ah," said the artist when Rachel met him again, "I have laid aside my brushes. I knew you were coming. I am too happy for work to-day."

"I am glad you are happy," said Rachel, quietly.

"I feel like a child," he answered; "I should like to play on the sands, and laugh with the waves, do anything a happy child might do."

"Do you feel related to all?" Rachel asked.

"Ay," he answered, "to the waves that kiss the shore, to the rocks, the earth, humanity, and the angels that sing in heaven. Heaven! Ah," and touching his breast, he said: "heaven is here. It is always here, if hell do not usurp its place."

He knelt, and taking up pebbles held them in his hands, saying: "These are messages to me. The world is a message. Glorified humanity! Holy God! Oh my soul, look and live!"

He raised his hands on high. "I would embrace all. My soul is infinite! Eternity is now. I seem to have lost all consciousness of self; I feel I am an invisible fluid, floating round with all humanity, all creation. My spirit is everywhere, and, strange as it may seem, with this submerging of self I have risen to great heights. I am great. I am Spirit."

Rachel stopped and looked at him with the full light of her deep eyes.

"That is right," he said, "look into my soul; see how it embraces yours, how it greets all souls. This is a prophecy—every beautiful thought we have, every good deed we do, are but prophecies; it lies in our power to make them fulfillments in this life. This would be the millennium, and it remains with us whether we will have it sooner or later. God himself will not bring it about till we are willing."

"How did you attain this?" asked Rachel.

"Why rehearse the story?" replied the artist. "No one can have the same experience. This one thing remember—I WAS WILLING TO BE FREE. How I have longed for Freedom! Freedom of body and soul!

"'Build thee more stately mansions, O my soul,
    As the swift seasons roll!
Leave thy low-vaulted past!
Let each new temple, statelier than the last,
Shut thee from heaven with a dome more vast,
    Till thou at length art free,
Leaving thy outgrown shell by life's unresting sea.'"

A beautiful picture they made—Rachel robed in white, her troubled face turned toward the sea; he, with a look of peace, seemed transfigured as the sunlight fell around them.

CHAPTER THIRTY-FOURTH.

> The quality of Mercy is not strain'd;
> It droppeth as the gentle rain from heaven,
> Upon the place beneath. It is twice bles'd;
> It blesseth him that gives and him that takes."
> —Shakespeare.

"Shall the Indian tell the English lord, that which has moved his soul more than all he has seen and heard in the great village?"

"Pray tell me, Garangula," answered Lord Carleton.

"The Indian was standing near a great dwelling-place. Not far away was a bridge. A stream flowed beneath it. Many people were going in the dwelling-place. The Indian went in with them. A grand man stood up and spoke to the people. His eyes looked as if he knew the way to the Happy Hunting-Grounds. He was not as tall as the English lord, but as he spoke he grew taller till he seemed a giant. He leaned forward and made motions, and his voice was like the music of the winds on the plains.

"Garangula could not understand what this great man said to the people, but he knew he was begging them to do a noble deed. Garangula arose and listened. He must stand, while near that man. Garangula felt strange. He wanted to go with this great Chieftain, who was calling on his tribe. If he would take Garangula with him, he would do anything the big Chief told him.

"Big Chief was grand. He looked like a great tree in the forest. He spoke on and on, growing more and more like a giant, his voice making stronger music. Garangula trembled. He must go with the great Chieftain. The Indian forgot where he was, and looked around for his bow and arrow and knife—Ay! Ay!"— his eyes flashed fire. "Garangula was ready to scalp, if the big Chief said." The Indian's voice ran into that musical guttural known only to the savage.

"Garangula looked around, everyone was still. They did not understand the Chief wanted them to do anything. But the Indian could not listen any longer without helping him. When the big Chief leaned forward, stretched out his arms and spoke strong again, Garangula took off his turban, and gave one long cry. He sprang from the dwelling-place, then ran on, to the banks of the stream, leaped into the water and swam many miles before he knew.

"*Nah saghalie oleman kull stik!*" he exclaimed.

Garangula's tall form quivered with excitement. Lord Carleton looked at him more and more astonished. Slowly he repeated the Indian's last words, translating them: "Oh, high old oak of the forest!"

A light broke over his face.

"Gladstone, by Jove!" and he clasped Garangula's hand.

"If the Grand Old Man had such followers as you, the Irish question would soon be settled."

CHAPTER THIRTY-FIFTH.

"Be ye therefore perfect, even as your Father which is in heaven is perfect."

NAMORA and Rachel had met again. They walked by the sea. Soon the artist approached them; his face lighted with joy at the sight of Namora, and he said: "I have prayed to see thee again."

Rachel looked surprised—she had not heard them speak of each other.

The artist said, with enthusiasm: "We spoke of miracles when last we were together. Would you repeat what you then told me? I wish this fair, troubled girl to hear," and he smiled benignantly at Rachel.

"There are no miracles," Namora replied.

"Christ performed no miracles. He obeyed The Law and the results astonished the people."

"The Law? Ah, what is The Law?" asked Rachel.

"It is Love," answered Namora.

"How may we learn The Law?" Rachel inquired.

"By forgetting self."

"And how may one do this?"

"By recognizing that all are one in the Father."

"But," Rachel said, anxiously, "suppose I cannot grasp that—what then must I do?"

"Live to help all men," replied Namora. "That is the only way to love God and grow into the recognition of the Father. It cannot be by the letter. It must be done in the spirit."

CHAPTER THIRTY-SIXTH.

> "Ye shall have a song as in the night when a holy solemnity is kept, and gladness of heart as when one goeth forth with a pipe to come into the mountain of the Lord, to the mighty one of Israel,"
> Isaiah, 30. 29.

LORD CARLETON paused a moment at the half-open door, unable to resist the deep music of the voice that slowly and patiently spelled the words: "S-o t-h-a-t i-t s-e-e-m-e-d N-i-g-h-t l-i-s-t-e-n-e-d i-n t-h-e g-l-e-n-s." The voice was stilled in the thought. Then it continued spelling, not laboriously but slowly:

"'And Noon upon the Mountains; yea! they write,
The evening stood between them like some maid,
Celestial, love-struck, rapt; the smooth-rolled clouds
Her braided hair; the studded stars the pearls
And diamonds of her coronal; the moon
Her forehead jewel, and the deepening dark,
Her woven garments. 'Twas her close-held breath——'"

The voice ended in a long-drawn breath, half a sigh, as if the soul were too full for utterance.

Lord Carleton could not forego the pleasure of interrupting the scene; he longed to hear Garangula speak his thoughts in words — it was the first book he had known him to attempt reading.

"Ah," said the Indian, the rapt expression breaking into a smile of gladness as Lord Carleton entered. "Ah, this is the voice of the Great Spirit. And Garangula, the Indian, listens."

Lord Carleton glanced at the book, and was surprised to find the lines he had heard, were more than half through the volume.

"Have you read — 'listened' — to all that?" He turned the leaves from the first.

"Garangula has listened to all of it."

"When could you have done this?"

"The Indian awakes in the night-time and listens. 'Tis then he hears best. The Voice speaks louder to him and he understands. Sometimes Garangula rises when the first light comes through the trees, and steals softly there and listens."

Lord Carleton looked at the handsomely bound volume and thought it one from his own library, till his eye caught sight of something that flashed. He took the book from Garangula's hand and looked at it wonderingly. Brilliant jewels had been dextrously fastened in the heavy morocco leather.

Garangula divined Lord Carleton's thoughts and said: "Garangula was passing a place. He stopped to look at the pictures. His eye fell on great rows of books. That one was lying open before him. Garangula bent over and listened. Soon a man came to take it, but Garangula said: 'The Indian wishes this. He will pay great money for it,' and he poured out gold, then looked at the man to see if he might have it. He looked strangely at Garangula and pushed the gold from him. Garangula was sorrowful. He thought the man would not part with it. But he made the Indian joyful; he took it and looked closely at the place where Garangula had listened, then gave it to him. Garangula put it close under his robe, pointed to the gold and left.

"Garangula set these jewels in the book.

His father gave them to him. The Indian feels sorry, because the man can never find another like this. When Garangula has listened a long time, he will take it to him."

He looked at the book caressingly and said: "But Garangula loves it."

"Oh well, Garangula," replied Lord Carleton, "I think you may keep it. If we can find the man, I will send him another."

"The English lord could not. There is no other."

Lord Carleton smiled. "Have you looked to see who wrote this book which pleases you so?"

"This is not a book," said the Indian, positively, as he took the volume from Lord Carleton's hands. "Garangula tells thee, English lord, that he *listens* to this and he hears the Voice of the Great Spirit." He crossed his hands on the book and held it to his breast.

"How pleased Sir Arnold would be, to hear that 'The Light of Asia' is the Voice of the Great Spirit, and my Garangula 'listens'," he said with a smile.

CHAPTER THIRTY-SEVENTH.

> "Which are a shadow of things to come; but the body is of Christ."
> Col. ii. 6.

It was Easter Sunday. They were walking through the cloisters, back and forth, both silent, Lord Carleton thinking of the monks who had striven to reach heaven from those dark cells—Garangula listening to the great organ.

Lord Carleton did not wish to enter the church until the service ended, lest his companion should hear something to disturb him. They went in as the audience dispersed.

The tones of the organ grew deeper and deeper, the strains more heavenly..... angels were ascending and descending....then came a triumphal shout, "Christ is risen!"

The last notes echoed along the arches.... died away in silence.... the sunlight burst from a cloud, and like a holy baptism fell on the departing worshipers. Lord Carleton and the Indian were alone in the great temple of the dead.

The tones of "Christ Is Risen," floated back and filled the sanctuary with a mystic holiness. In exaltation, Garangula closed his eyes and threw back his head. The light fell on his upturned face.... The "mystic holiness" gathered about him. Lord Carleton, standing apart, looked at him as the light touched his brow—
"Ye gods! What a wondrous face!" he murmured.

The Indian slowly opened his eyes, looked at the arches—at the long lines, "reminding one of the soul's hunger;" then at the windows, over whose pictured saints the sun was casting a halo, and said: "This is like a forest with the glory of the Great Spirit shining through!"

He gazed at the human symbols of goodness and greatness, and said: "Ah, there is something here that makes Garangula feel like drawing his mantle around him and falling on the ground, his face touching the earth."

"Does he feel, I wonder," thought Lord Carleton, "that he is within our 'holy sepulchre', our sanctuary, our grand old Westminster? So be it. He has more reverence for both God and man than his friend. I am humbled again."

He went nearer, drew the Indian's arm through his and passed from the Abbey, not speaking till they reached Westminster Bridge.

The soft light of the setting sun played on the Thames....The Westminster Palace cast its dark shadow on the waters....Lord Carleton thought, "Christ is risen!"

The Indian said softly: "The Great Spirit is over all!"

CHAPTER THIRTY-EIGHTH.

> "And the princes, governors and captains, and the king's counselors, being gathered together, saw these men, upon whose bodies the fire had no power, nor was a hair of their head singed, neither were their coats changed, nor the smell of fire had passed on them."
>
> Daniel 3. 27.

IN that sequestered spot in the valley, shut in from the rough winds of the sea, Uncle Jonah's home lay peaceful and still. A full moon looked down, glinting here and there the ancient sandstone of the cottage, lighting up the deep, mullioned windows, touching the dark green of the ivy that shaded the porch and climbed to the thatched roof. About the old stone well, the shadows played and peeped down into the cool, clear water that reflected the rude carving of some swain hundreds of years ago. Close by, stood a grand old horse chestnut with spreading branches. Fruit trees sent their showers of pink and white blossoms to the ground. Wild flowers grew beside the lonely country road that stretched away in the moorlands. The ivy bent its green to the moss-grown wall that enclosed the garden; clematis grew about the gate and touched the sweet-brier that clamored for its place in the ruins of the old wall. In a far-away hidden corner, the violets looked out timidly at the moonbeams. The lilacs bloomed in great profusion and sent their perfume on the air. The moonlight and perfumes and colors sought each other. Clouds of incense seemed to rise from the earth, and peace was over all.

Rachel lay sleeping, the moonbeams kissing her as they stole through the white roses that enframed her window. Her face was less troubled than in the past .... Peace was coming to its home! She smiled .... angels were near.

A light brighter than the moonbeams flashed .... again and again still brighter. A low, uneasy, crackling sound disturbed the stillness. Rachel moved; her arms fell on her bosom, she still smiled. The light flashed stronger, the sounds grew distinct, like the sigh of a coming storm.... A man's voice was heard, then a piercing cry of "Fire!" as clouds of smoke enveloped the stairway.

"Oh, my lamb! My child! Must you perish?" and the old man in frenzy, rushed to the stairs—the flames drove him back.

The fair sleeper had risen and stood by the window, the smile not wholly faded from her face. She looked up at the sky—the moon shone as if no tragedies were being enacted. The roar of the sea in the distance mingled with that of the flames, which grew more furious each moment. She turned a peaceful face toward her terrified friends, and said: "All is well. I am not afraid."

Great forked flames, striving to reach their victim, shot up from the back of the house in demoniacal fury. Rachel's face grew more divine.... Another moment and the flames would encircle her....

Then came a silence vast and awful.... The flames seemed stayed. Rachel felt arms about her and thought an angel had come to lead her on the way. A rope was drawn quickly and securely around her waist, but she did not realize this—only the tender arms. Her soul was apparently reaching out into another life. Some one said: "Fear not." A moment more, and she was clasped in the arms of her friends. The flames burst forth from below and swept on.

Rachel had now fully awakened to a sense of the danger, through which she had passed unharmed. An inexplicable look came into her face as she gazed at the burning house. Above the roar of the flames, she heard a voice clear and distinct:

"LIGHT IS GREATER THAN FIRE."

CHAPTER THIRTY-NINTH.

> "Who is as the wise man? and who knoweth the interpretation of a thing? a man's wisdom maketh his face to shine........"
> Ecclesiastes 8. 1.

"OH! whar is my missus?" in great distress asked Aunt Dinah of the watchman who stood at the door of the theatre in the Strange Palace.

"She is there," answered the watchman, looking toward the entrance that led to the stage. "Your mistress has pleased the people, I heard the applause but a few minutes ago."

"She's not thar," cried Aunt Dinah, wringing her hands. "I hab jes' cum frum dar, an' I couldn't find her nowhar, an' de people looked strange an' wus agoin' away. Oh, Lawd, ole Dinah beliebes de world am cumin' to an end dis night."

"Stop, my good woman," said the watchman, "tell me what troubles you. Let me help you."

"Ole Dinah's heart am broke," said the weeping servant. "My purty lamb, my little Wanda am wid de angels; dey hab cum an' tuk her home."

"Why, when did this happen?" asked the watchman, sympathetically.

"Ole Dinah had put her to bed dis ebnin'," she replied, "an' sot by her an' sung. Arter while, I begun to nod, an' I don't know no mo', tel I woke up wid a start, an' looked for de baby. She wus a-standin' still in de cradle. Ole Dinah was skeered—though she didn't look sick—jes' strange like. I went slowly up to her—she wus a-smilin' jes' like I'm dreamed de angels smile, an' dar cum a light on her face dat made ole Dinah mo' an' mo' afeard. Den all ub a suddin, dar cum sich a look as I'm neber seen on de face ub mortal creetur. Jes' as I got to her, she sorter trimbled all ober an' fell. Ole Dinah snatched her up quick an' felt ub her heart; it neber did beat enny mo'. I called fur sumbody to cum, but nobody answered—de baby's muther wus here," and Aunt Dinah burst into tears.

The strange lights burned low in the Egyptian Theatre. Incense floated in from a temple not far away. On either side of the stage, the sphinx still sat. In their mystic repose they were saying, as they had done for thousands of years: "We know the beginning. We know the end."

The excitement in the vast audience was so intense, there seemed to be one great, deep heart-throb. The orchestra played a low, weird strain. A voice sang—a voice so rich and powerful, yet such an intonation that some whispered: "It is a soul crying for light!" But many were electrified. Then, the voice grew tremulous and seemed calling to someone as it found its way through a labyrinth—it came nearer and nearer, growing fuller and stronger till with one triumphant note, it cried: "Found!"

Zulona stood before them—a Queen of Song.

The words of that wonderful opera fell from lips that seemed 'neath a spell. The notes rose and swelled, filling the theatre..........the tone suddenly ceased—Zulona turned pale, every nerve quivering as she stared at the dome of the theatre. No one breathed, no one moved.

Then wildly, madly, she clutched at her throat. A tone rose and swept on, as though trying to reach the stars. The voice was silent again — the singer grew deadly pale, her eyes became transfixed. The audience strove to see that which their vision could not discern.

Zulona opened her lips... the voice died away in a whisper.... Dazed and hopeless, she went from the theatre....

"Yes, yes, I understood;" she whispered, standing beside the cradle of her dead child. "And yet, oh God!—I was ambitious. Oh my baby, my baby!"

Her body swayed, she fell senseless.

After a time, Zulona opened her eyes; they were sunken, her face haggard—she had grown an old woman within a few hours. She looked at the lifeless form, and said as though to someone, yet she was alone—"Take her away! Another sight of her dear, sweet face would drive me mad! Great God! I thought I loved nothing but ambition—I know differently now. That is a small thing compared to the beautiful child gone forever from this life. From this life? Is there then another? I have not thought so, but now, I want to know that my baby lives again! If I could be assured, there would be some hope left! But alas! I do not know this—no man can tell me, and woe, unutterable woe is the doubt! It seems to me the very stars in heaven are wheeling wildly about and clashing together. Oh, this black, black night! This never-to-be-forgotten darkness that surrounds me. I see not one single ray of light, or hope, or joy any more forever. Forever and forever! How that word clashes through my whole being and leaves my brain burning! Truly this is my Garden of Gethsemane!"

Aunt Dinah, with tear-stained eyes, waited by the door.

"No; go away," the sorrowing mother said. "You are kind, but do not come near me! Leave me alone with my sorrow! Perhaps the time may come when I can bear to look on another's face, but not now—not now." The words died in a sob. "Let no one come near me this night. And in the morning"—she shivered—"let someone take her away. My baby! Oh my beautiful baby!" she murmured softly.

At midnight, the faithful servant found her lying with her face on the floor.

In obedience to a rite she had witnessed, Aunt Dinah placed candles around the dead body. The suffering mother still lay prostrate. Soon she raised her head—the lights startled her. She drew back, then stood looking intently. Was there not some other light than the candles? The baby's face was illumined. Was it speaking to her? She moved nearer and bent over the couch. A sudden darkness swept between them. Then—or was it imagination?... From out the darkness a horrible spectre evolved.....slowly, step by step, she moved back, her eyes glaring in horror, her bloodless lips frozen....Feebly she raised her limp hands to shut out the vision, then the arms were flung madly behind the head, and a wild laugh echoed through the room.

"Ha! ha! You come to-night! This night of all the years since I banished your spirit—that mine might—be—free! Yes, yes, I committed the deed," the words came in shrieks; her eyes were ablaze.

"With—this—hand I did it—!" She swiftly clasped it to her bosom, and with a mad laugh cried: "Oh hand, I kiss thee! Thou didst it for my freedom! Ha! ha! Thou spectre! Damnable in death as in life. Leave me!"

Gradually the scene changed; the darkness gave place to a soft light, a light that grew and filled the room. Zulona became more calm. The eyes looked out with a wisdom unknown to them, as she moved beside the child and knelt. She heard the whisperings of a voice, tender and inspiring, "Freedom comes from Within!" it said.

The candles burned more brightly. The mother knelt lower.

CHAPTER FORTIETH.

"Every valley shall be exalted, and every mountain and hill shall be made low and the crooked shall be made straight, and the rough places plain."

Isaiah, 40. 4.

On the morning after Wanda's death, Garangula was in the Strange Palace. He said: "Tell the beautiful pale-face that Garangula, the Indian, would take the little papoose and bear it away to the forests, and bury it after the fashion of his own people."

He waited, as if for reply, then continued: "The Great Spirit sent Garangula to do this. When the sun has gone down, and the lamp is hung high in the heavens, the Indian will come for the little white papoose."

Saying this, he glided from the room, all the

native Indian appearing now that his emotions were awakened. There was not Zulona's influence, nor that of Lord Carleton—it was the dusky mother coming to the surface. Every movement, every tone was Indian, and his listeners looked at each other in wondering silence.

When the day had gone, and the moon hung high in the heavens, Garangula entered the Egyptian Apartments. Round the bier were young girls robed in white; about their heads veils were confined with wreaths of white blossoms. They made room for Garangula. With closed eyes and bowed head, he moved slowly around the body three times in a circle, chanting one of his native songs. Then he spoke with a mournful cadence:

"Garangula, the Indian, sends this message to the sorrowing pale-face. O beautiful, sad-eyed mother, Garangula will take thy baby and bury it after the manner of the red man. The Indian doth promise thee this: Those who have gone on a journey to the Happy Hunting-Grounds, will watch over thy papoose. O Star-Eyed-One, farewell!"

The Indian took his place beside the bier; again he bowed his head and crossed his hands on his breast.

The moon shone through the trees and fell on the people of the Strange Palace, who stood with uncovered heads. The white robed maidens, nine in number, walked with soft, measured touch to the Indian's chant. Aunt Dinah and the faithful dog followed. Through the gates of the Strange Palace the procession moved softly, musically, on to the forests, in whose bosom they laid Zulona's child to sleep.

The Lamp o' the Night whispered softly to the Indian that another day had begun. Still he stood by the little grave; the dog at his side looked up questioningly.

"Garangula must go deeper into the forests," he spoke, in his own language. "Must go deep into the forests and seek that he has lost. Garangula does not understand"—a look of confusion passed o'er his face—"but something has gone from the Indian, and he must find it."

Garangula went into the forests; the dog laid down by the grave.

CHAPTER FORTY-FIRST.

> "Farewell, a long farewell to all my greatness,
> This is the state of man; to-day he puts forth
> The tender leaves of hope, to-morrow blossoms,
> And bears his blushing honors thick upon him,
> The third day comes a frost, a killing frost;
> And, he thinks, good easy man, full surely
> His greatness is unripening—nips his roots,
> And then he falls as I do.................."
>
> Shakespeare.

"While the morning was yet young," a woman robed in gray, was nearing the Strange Palace. She seemed borne by some invisible power, there was so little effort in every movement.

Within the Egyptian Apartments, a pale woman sat by the table, writing. A curious, old Egyptian lamp, its oil well nigh spent, cast faint light on the paper. The woman was dressed for traveling. Her hand nervously glided over the paper as she wrote:

Dear Aunt Dinah—I am going away from the Strange Palace.

I leave this money for you. Go back to the old home and wait for me. Sometime, I will return—have faith in me. Good-bye, Aunt Dinah, my faithful nurse—the only friend I have in all the world. Forgive me for leaving you. ZULONA.

The letter was sealed and stamped with a monogram that had not been used for a long time.

She arose. The lamp had gone out. The mantle was drawn more closely about her, the better to disguise herself. She paused a moment—every line on her face spoke of a purpose difficult to fathom. Clasping a small packet, she stole from the room, and stealthily crept through the long halls and intricate passages of the Strange Palace—on to the broad avenue. She had nearly reached the gates before she thought of their being locked—Heaven forbid! and they would not open again for six days; the thought was like a stab—she held her breath. Lo! the gates noiselessly opened. She passed through, unheeding the miracle—the new resolution so filled her.

But a few steps had been taken, when in front of her she saw Namora. Zulona said humbly: "Help me! I am willing to learn of you now."

She of the Light looked at her with sympathy and love, and the two went on.

CHAPTER FORTY-SECOND

"But there shall not an hair of your head perish."
Luke, 21-18.

AFTER the night of the vision, Leota the Indian maiden, studied and worked steadily onward. Her teachers became proud of her attainments. True, she had lost something of the stillness she possessed five years before—the deep, sustained breath which gives freedom, was no longer hers. In compensation, the curves of her waist were deeper and more at variance with shoulders and hips—this was part of her education. Her tones were not so pure but her "sentences were grammatical"; this, too, was satisfactory.

Ofttimes they told her she would uplift her

people, when she returned as a missionary. These words and the vision sustained her.

The time came at last, when she stood before an audience, and said parting words to her classmates.....

Ten moons had grown full and paled, since Leota returned to the Reservation to uplift her people.

* * * * * * * *

It was a night like the one when Garangula slept in front of her father's wigwam. She was alone upon a cliff. The stars moved slowly above her....The mountains towered majestically around her....The stillness was awesome. With a voice calm as the stars she spoke:

"Great Spirit, Leota, the Indian maiden, has no home this side the Happy Hunting-Grounds. No place among the pale-faces. No place with the red man. O Great Spirit! The Indian maiden asks one boon of Thee. Let her spirit go to Garangula, and help him with our people."

She bowed her head and folded her arms on her breast, then flung herself from the steep. Lo! midway the precipice her body was caught up by fire.... three times it circled, then vanished.

Far above, an ethereal substance swept on into the Great Light.

וְהַבַּ֙יִת֙ בְּהִבָּ֣נֹת֔וֹ אֶֽבֶן־שְׁלֵמָ֥ה מַסָּ֖ע נִבְנָ֑ה וּמַקָּב֤וֹת וְהַגַּרְזֶן֙ כָּל־כְּלִ֣י בַרְזֶ֔ל לֹֽא־נִשְׁמַ֥ע בַּבַּ֖יִת בְּהִבָּנֹתֽוֹ

3 Kings, 6-7.

IN the midst of a great city stood a Temple called The Beautiful. Broad halls there were, with great arched doorways, but no doors save one. Windows pictured the Glory of God, and when the sun through them shone, all things were Illumined.

The Temple was of an architecture unknown to men, and they called it wondrous. Men profane, looked on it and thought it music, poetry and sculpture. Others said: "No, it is Religion." And yet a third, who deemed himself wiser than the rest, said: "It is Art and Religion."

Artists looked on it, and all things sensuous were lost in symbols. Art had a meaning anew.

Lovers of Good on it gazed. Through Truth they saw Beauty.

So great the architecture it seemed thousands of years old. Some believed it had been builded in a night-time, that God's messengers had come and built it whilst they slept.

Soft tones like the whisperings of angels floated throughout that Temple. On its façade was a great clock that marked the hours by music.... music that made many a weary traveler pause as he listened to tones that suggested new thoughts of time.

IT WAS ETERNITY NOW.

"IN THE GREAT FOREVER GOOD CREATES."

Golden gates, wrought with a curious design, enclosed the Temple. Each time a chord was touched from the great clock, the gates swung open. Like the statue of old, it struck the first chord at sunrise, and the gates swung to and fro till the sun went down. Then opened not before the dawn of another day.

And as the gates opened, men looked and wondered, and wondering, entered. Then moved by aught they knew not, they desired Understanding.

Within the Temple were three chambers more wondrous still.

Over the first was writ....Silence. Within that sacred place, the ways of the sons of men were not. And yet, one must listen....to catch the whisperings of the angels.

O sacred Chamber of Silence, that angels builded in the night-time! How can one describe thee unto men! It is still there within the Temple Beautiful that stands in the midst of a great city....You must listen would you catch the whisperings of the angels.

Between the Chambers of Silence and Truth was a veil. To some it disappeared. Yet many looked and understood not its meaning.

The third chamber was not so peaceful as the others. And the way that led thereto was not long but intricate....winding passages intersected the corridor, and many peoples lost their way.

A vast, white chamber it was, and very beautiful. From the portal there were steps that led to a living picture, with a halo around it.

To some it appeared a beautiful Madonna floating in the sunlight, above a scythe that glistened in the golden grain. The babe she held in her arms, smiled as he stretched out his hands toward the sheaves. A peasant paused in his work now and then to look up at the holy Madonna.

O Madonna of the Scythe! O Holy Mary! How can I tell of thee unto men! I cannot. And I weep it is thus.... In a far away temple—the Temple of Motherhood it lives.

BUT YOU MUST HAVE WISDOM TO SEE IT.

Far and wide spread the fame of the Temple, till sons of men from all nations of the earth journeyed thither.

And in the night-time when the great world slept, a white-robed Priestess went in and out of the Temple, like the Vestas of old, who kept the sacred fires of Rome burning night and day. So radiant was her face, and peaceful, that when she stood in the doorway of the Temple, and looked out in the night as she sometimes did, the sight of her moved one to awe, and the watchman would bow his head and cry out the hour.

Song in that temple was divine. All force became Glorified. Beings who tarried therein were illumined. They knew God.

On the walls hung a wonderful chart. From the base there grew a combination of angles and curves. These became spirals and finally converged into a Great Circle. In its centre was the word—Truth.

Along the base line was writ, Economy. From the Spirals there swept up a mysterious figure bearing the name of Freedom. This reached out and connected itself with the Great Circle round which was writ, Power.

From the figure of Freedom a ray of light strove to pass in a straight line, but there gathered about it a brilliance as of millions of suns. And its identity was lost.

Radiating from Truth was the wonderful trinity — Economy, Freedom, Power. It embraced all the relations of life.

Lawgivers interpreted it and saw the true Political Economy, realizing Universal Brotherhood. They recognized that the true understanding of the principle in creation brings Freedom. And that Freedom gives all Power.

Artists looked on it and said: "Art is no longer a mystic incarnation."

All the world received instruction. They learned there was no bondage save violation of Law. And no Freedom save obedience to Law. That "through Love Wisdom is found." Therefore, unto Love all things are possible.

וְסֻכָּה תִּהְיֶה לְצֵל־יוֹמָם מֵחֹרֶב וּלְמַחְסֶה
וּלְמִסְתּוֹר מִזֶּרֶם וּמִמָּטָר

Isaiah, 4=6.

THE Temple Beautiful still stood in the midst of a great city. The clock continued to mark off the hours. The music flowed on. Echoes were heard anon far away from the gates.

The white-robed Priestess had reached the highest development of Woman. Intuition was complete. She was surrounded by a great light, and when she gave forth knowledge this grew brighter, until at times all Identity was lost.

She spake unto the women, telling them they were the Wisdom Principle in Creation. And that principle would unfold all Power, bringing Peace on earth. The world would not attain

Perfect Expression until Woman became the shrine of Wisdom and Love.

And it came to pass, that while the sons of men from all nations of the earth gathered together in the Temple, they brought offerings and laid them at the gates. The rich man left bonds of great estates that he might enter the Chamber of Silence. Women brought jewels. A sad-eyed mother softly laid a little white robe with the others. A packet of letters, yellow with time, were found hidden in a casket. Those who begged, gave coppers at the gates. Hard hands laid down a whole life's labor. The most beautiful gave up her conquests, the statesman his ambition, the warrior his pride, the poor their poverty.

It was whispered the time of Peace was drawing nigh. Still the high Priestess, whom they called Rachel, went in and out of the Temple, and spake unto the people.

"The Christmastide draweth nigh," she said, one holy day. "Retreat within the Bethlehem of thine own souls. Let the Christ speak. Let the light from the East shine above the Judean hills of all the earth."

She told them what the light was—the sweet, beautiful life, so divine yet simple, clothed in a glory unknown before. Through this pure Life the Great Mystery was solved. They learned to become Brothers in Christ, and through this, understood the At-one-ment with the Father.

The multitude sang praises: "Glory to God in the highest, and on earth peace, good will towards men!"

Echoes came back from the uttermost parts of the earth, "The light is about us."

מָחִ֧יתִי כָעָ֛ב פְּשָׁעֶ֖יךָ וְכֶעָנָ֣ן חַטֹּאותֶ֑יךָ
שׁוּבָ֥ה אֵלַ֖י כִּ֥י גְאַלְתִּֽיךָ

Isaiah, 44, 22.

IN the great city where stood the Temple Beautiful, the people assembled, inquiring, "Who is this come whose creations have breath? Whose song reveals the divinity of man, because the respirations are from the depths of the soul? Art may now become the embodiment of a spiritual truth—the Truth that shows the beauty and power of man when he shall be an 'embodied soul and ensouled body'."

There was not only a culmination of all that had been in Art, but a Prophecy. The artist could enact the Prophetic Ideal. "But lo!" said the critics, with troubled countenance, "there is no Prophetic Ideal."

Startling fact! Terrible revelation!

"Can it be," said they, "that we are so poor? Surely we might find that we seek in all the centuries have hoarded."

Still troubled, they said: "Is it true that as we are passing through the realm of life which leads to all Beauty, and no longer care to have crime, and the misconception of passion portrayed on the stage—no longer care to see what we have been; but desire earnestly to know our highest selves, and have shadowed forth to us what we may be, even in this life—there is no drama or opera in which this can be done?"

They were aghast at the revelation! "False reasoners!" cried one who had wisdom. "Blind are we not to know this truth, which the simplest thing in nature would teach us, if we understood the alphabet: Every color in all this beautiful world has its correspondence, yea, every tint and sound.

"If one hath arisen who can foretell what humanity may become, an opportunity will be allotted.

"Then why doubt? Listen to the harmonies of God's world, and wait...."

While they waited there came a voice from a distant land. One who desired not to be heralded.

* * *

No curtain fell....the scene continued the same. At the end of the first act, the applause rang, to be taken up again like waves of music; but the singer made no recognition....Approbation gave place to cries; women tore off their jewels and flung them at her feet. The wonderful artist, the glorified being, knelt, and from the jewels, took a spray of olive and placed it in her bosom.

The light from that far-off time had found its way through the darkness of all the ages, and again revealed itself unto men   The stars grew brighter and moved with more perfect rhythm. The "spheres chorused with her, shouting the pæans of victory." It was not song, and yet it was the highest expression of Song.

"Victory!" cried Zulona, leaving the stage.

"Nay, Peace," said She of the Holy Light.

CHAPTER FORTY-THIRD.

> "Light is sown for the righteous, for the upright in heart."
> Psalm 98. 11.

THERE was a great *fête* in Rome. A master had risen among them, but they knew him not. They could learn nothing concerning him save the most romantic story. Who was he? Whence had he come? A *fête* given in honor of one they did not know!

The rooms set apart for the two great works, were thronged with people. The excitement could be compared to nothing but a political crisis in olden times. They called for the master to come forth and be crowned. Artists from all Italy came, and the fame went to other countries.

The statues were of bronze. Critics said they were greater than anything Michael Angelo had done. The artist had combined grace and force with an indefinable spirituality.

"If I could only see them!" said Lord Carleton, as he and Lady Carleton stood among the crowd. "From the description, one at least, must be a statue of Garangula; and, Elise, my heart tells me it is, and that through this I shall find my friend."

They waited a long time with impatience—the crowd slowly moved near and Lord Carleton caught a glimpse.

"My long sought Garangula!" he cried. As the dignity and majesty of the statue grew upon him, tears were in his eyes.

"How well I know that poise!" he said, at length. "I do not wonder the Italians are wild over them. But where is Garangula? You are not hearing a word I am saying, Lady Carleton, but I pardon you. Much as I admired him, I did not dream he was so handsome. Look! there is the other statue. The same form. But

I cannot stay; my impatience to see Garangula grows, now that I feel he may be near."

They retraced their way slowly through the crowd. "And think, dear," Lord Carleton continued, "it was Garangula who led me to you. I have not yet learned what 'obeying the Law of Succession' means, but I am content that you are now Lady Carleton."

As they walked down the broad, marble steps, they passed a man talking in suppressed tones to his servant.

"Damnable fool!" he said. "Were you not sent here to watch Garangula? Where has he gone? Did I not tell you to overshadow him day and night? Cursed be my star that took me from Rome! Where is Garangula, faithless servant?"

"Oh, sir, your servant knows not," he answered tremblingly.

"What have you been doing?"

"I know not how to tell it, sir. I attempted to find my way to him, but could not."

"Idiot, did you not have my directions?"

"Ay, sir, and tried to use them," replied the

frightened servant. "But each time—I know not what happened, I lost my way. Then I hired a guide, and he too, grew confused; at last, I became unconscious, and was taken to my lodgings, and knew nothing more until this morning, when they gave me your dispatch."

The light fell aslant the bronze statues. Mazaro stood beside them; his eyes were set, his limbs grown rigid.

With effort, his hand found its way to his bosom, and drew forth a dagger. Black clouds of smoke burst from his breast and moved in downward spirals. Demons gathered about him.

"Garangula is within the Great Circle," they hissed in his ear, and laughed demoniacally.

The smoke grew blacker, the spirals smaller, swifter and stronger; then swept backward with greater force, each wave of smoke bearing horrible discords, till all the air seemed filled with voices of the damned.

The dagger was slowly raised—the evil spirits pressed closer and closer around him, the black clouds enveloping them. The knife descended, and Mazaro's lifeless body fell at the foot of Garangula's statue.

CHAPTER FORTY-FOURTH.

"And they thirsted not when he led them through the deserts: he caused the waters to flow out of the rock for them......"

Isaiah, 47. 21.

It was weeks before Lord Carleton succeeded in getting any clue whatever to the Indian. At last, the story came out. Only one man in Rome had known him, and he willingly gave the limited information.

It was in this wise: It chanced one day that an American artist was in Switzerland, enjoying the beauties of that land, when standing at the foot of a mountain, he saw an Indian descending. The artist, wonderstruck, cried aloud—"Ye gods! are ye come to visit the earth once more?"

The Indian slowly descended. He seemed in

harmony with the universe and moved with the rhythm of the stars.

The artist approached him. Garangula looked at him a moment, then said: "Let thou and Garangula journey together. The Great Spirit wills it."

The man felt half afraid of so strange a character, but his love of beauty overcame, and the two journeyed to the Eternal City.

The artist, who was a sculptor, asked Garangula to sit for him.

The Indian replied: "The great Manito wills that Garangula sit for thee."

Day after day the sculptor worked, Garangula watching him with much interest, and while he watched, all his love of beauty seemed near its unfoldment. At times, his face swept out of its calm repose; there was a curious working of the muscles, and he murmured incoherently in the Indian language—"The Great Spirit is near—Garangula will know."

The sculptor was one of the artists who are slaves to their emotions. He often let the clay fall from his hands and sat dreaming of the great heroic action he would reproduce in marble.

Both the artist and the Indian grew by the association, although in a different way.

The Indian had a propitious environment. He was associated with a man who had great refinement of character, and whose feeling for art was quick, strong, and tender. Above all, some would say, he was in Rome, the Mecca whither artists journeyed in those days and laid their offerings. All places were Mecca to Garangula. He left offerings everywhere—if holy thoughts be prayers. Perhaps the holiest of these he gave to the sculptor's studio, which was an "idealization realized."

This studio was in the southwest corner of the ruins of the Diocletian Baths. The *Thermæ* of Diocletian, from which the *piazza* took its name, were once the largest in Rome. It is said the work of these great baths was done by condemned Christians, who, as they wrought, made the sign of the cross on the bricks. The cross is still to be seen as the bricks fall from the ruins. Perhaps the thoughts of the Christian martyrs hovered about the plaintive memorial of their faith, and still lingered among the ruins. It may be the harmony in the studio was partly due to this influence. Vines grew among the ruins, finding their way into every crevice, and falling down the sides of the building, concealed an arch above a flight of steps that led to a landing, this being enclosed by trelliswork and covered with vines. Pigeons flew in and out cooing softly.

But for the flight of steps and the landing, the ruins would have appeared unoccupied — so still and so peaceful were they. Standing by the fountain, with the sunlight falling around, the soft sky overhead, the memory of the cross — one unconsciously breathed a prayer.

These notes of beauty were only a foreshadowing of the music within, a prelude to be heard while ascending the steps. An arched door opened into a circular room, so solid and massive, it looked as if it had been hewn out of a gigantic rock.

From three points of the room vines ran up and twined around an odd candelabrum, making a picturesque effect. On the walls, were pictures without frames, so arranged that at a distance they seemed wonderful frescoes. A portrait bust or two in marble—but one closed his eyes and said: "Let me feel—I wish to see nothing more."

All was silent. The hum of the city did not reach there, save as something afar off, in which they had no part. Sweet incense from the past floated in through the one window that looked out on Rome, and brought an influence of hope and faith.

The bronze figure of Homer sat reading on the sands, taking thoughts back to the old Homeric days. Leaving this place, one went out into the world better than when he entered; better, because he knew the ideal could be realized. That was the key-note of the harmony.

This was Garangula's home. He refused to share the artist's apartments in the suburbs. At night, he slept on the stone floor over which rugs were thrown, or when the weather was warm he stayed on the landing.

Thither Garangula was led after his two years' sojourn among the mountains of Switzerland.

CHAPTER FORTY-FIFTH.

> "By Babel's streams we sat and wept,
> For memory still to Zion clung;
> The winds alone our harp-strings swept,
> That on the drooping willows hung."
> **Psalms 137. 1-2.**

WHEN Garangula left the grave of Zulona's child, he journeyed far to the land of the Swiss, and stayed in the "forests"—thus he called the mountains of Switzerland. "Garangula went on from these woods," he said, "till he came to lakes of beauty; beyond were the hills. The first at which Garangula tarried, reminded him of the home of his forefathers. While there, he found the rocky side of a hill on which a great lion was cut."

"Lucerne!" exclaimed the sculptor.

"Garangula felt strange as he looked at the

lion cut in the rock. He trembled and rushed away, crying: 'Garangula must find that which he has lost.'

"He went to the foot of the mountain where he lingered many months, sleeping on the ground, watching the lamp of the Great Spirit by night, and the clouds, the sky, and the sunlight by day.

"Once a storm raged among the hills and swept through the valleys, the fire of the Great Spirit sped in and out of the blackness. Noises, greater than thunder, echoed and gathered in strength till they seemed to unite in one mighty cry to the Great Spirit. Garangula bared his head, drew his mantle from his breast, and cried out.

"Then all grew still. Garangula listened and felt the Great Spirit heard his voice.

"One day when he was by the waters that surrounded long points of the forest, he saw many people coming up in canoes. They walked into a chapel near, and knelt. Garangula did not know what it meant. They told him it was Easter Sunday. Then he remembered the Lamp had hung in the sky twelve times since he and the English lord heard music on a day they called Easter. The Indian went in and knelt.

"A long time Garangula wandered. The hills and jagged rocks towered above him, solemn and grand. Garangula walked with bared head always.

"He came to a lake shaped like the Lamp looks when it has not hung long. He went on to a stream whose waters were blue as the sky. It was night—still Garangula walked, always by the water's edge. Many days he spent going up and down this stream. One night he saw lights shining on the water and in the distance a village. Garangula went there but did not tarry, he could not stay from the forests. Each morning Garangula felt the Great Spirit led him to the hills, the blue waters, and he journeyed till he came to a great valley. Above him rose the Everlasting Hill. He went up rugged places, through the clouds. At last he was above them, and the sun looked down where the white winds had fallen to rest.

"Garangula felt he was in the abode of the Great Spirit. He took off his sandals and stood still. Night came on—the Lamp hung out full and round. The Indian lay down on his face and slept. When the great morning was come Garangula awoke. She of the Holy Light stood before him. She looked toward the valley, and said: 'Go thy way thither; thou wilt know!'"

CHAPTER FORTY-SIXTH.

"And unto whatsoever house ye enter, say 'Peace be to this house.'"
Luke 10. 5.

THE sculptor wished to study his model. To do this, he took Garangula to places he thought would move him. He desired the Indian to see the best architecture and sculpture, hoping it would help him as well as Garangula. He builded wiser than he knew.

One day, after successful effort, the sculptor said: "No more work; let us to the Pantheon."

They passed the fountain, crossed *via Nazionale*, and went down narrow streets amid dirt and squalor, which happily one forgets as he looks up at the soft, blue sky.

Reaching the Capitoline Hill, the Indian

looked at the equestrian statue of Marcus Aurelius; he threw back his head; his nostrils dilated—a just tribute—the grand old Emperor seemed to respond; his imperial air heightened, and one felt the noble steed might leap down the steps and meet the barbarian with a neigh.

To most people, Rome was. To the Indian, Rome is. The spirit of poetry and beauty still lingers, is reflected from the sky, envelops the Alban Hills, and soars to the snowcapped mountains, comes back and whispers to him—"I was—I will be forever."

The Indian cannot revel in the past of bloody Rome. If there be thoughts of the monsters of that period still hovering about the Seven Hills, he does not attract them. Furthermore, this savage, like many another less ignorant and less holy, has perceptions there—he knows not how or why, and the very beauty consists in their being beyond analysis. It may be it is always so of the Spirit of Beauty, but one feels it more in Rome than elsewhere.

The majesty of the Pantheon rose before them. Through the blackened columns of the portico, the Indian saw the beauty and dignity within. He bowed his head and entered.

The sculptor followed curiously. A ceremony was taking place—an anniversary of the death of a potentate. A light falling from quaint holders filled with spirits, whose effect was not dispelled by the thousand candles that flamed and burned—the music, soft, low, and solemn, priests chanting the mass, the statues of saints looking down from their niches between Corinthian columns—all spoke to the Indian.

The last notes of the music grew softer and softer, the echoes came back through the centre of the dome and mingled with the sunshine, then died away. The people passed through the great doorway. All was still. The Indian moved where the catafalque had stood. He took off his turban, and looked up at the heavens, and said: "Until now the Indian doubted if the Great Manitou ever dwelt in a temple made by man. Mother," his face was that of a little child, "Mother, let Garangula hear thy voice; he believes thou art looking down on him now. Speak to thy child."

He closed his eyes and listened; clouds drifted over the opening, the light touched his head.

The sculptor gazed in wonder on his strange model from whom he could learn nothing, save that he belonged to the race of red men, and had come across the sea.

Softly stepping over the green moss on the old stones, Garangula went to the tomb of Raphael, and spelled the word that had no meaning to him. He slowly moved around the room, stopping before some stately altar. At last, he was by the doorway, speaking softly in the Indian language. When outside the gates, the Indian looked back.

"Tell Garangula of the people who built the Temple."

The sculptor, led by a fancy, wove romance with the truth. But Garangula was unmoved, and shook his head. Then the sculptor told him the true history of the Pantheon—that it was built by the pagans—thinking the Indian would not comprehend, he said "savages."

Garangula replied: "The Indian has often wondered the difference between the white man and the savage. Now he knows."

CHAPTER FORTY-SEVENTH.

"Except the Lord build the house, they labour in vain that build it."
Psalm cxxvii, 1.

GARANGULA and the sculptor walked in silence from the Pantheon till they came to a dingy, little restaurant. Garangula ate little; he sat listening to the soft, Italian language.

From the restaurant, the sculptor took Garangula to the Fountain of Trevi, the most beautiful in the world, despite its absurd sculpturing in marble, intended for a design. Truly Bernini's school sent forth disciples who perpetuated follies in marble, yet one forgives them as he stands beside the Fountain of Trevi to-night.

The Lamp of the Great Spirit lighted the dim and narrow streets of the Imperial City;

it made a fairy's home of the Palace of the Cæsars, flooded the Forum, and kissed the snowy fountain.

The Indian knelt and played with the waters. The sculptor told him the legends connected with the wonderful fountain. The Indian listened while he looked at the palace front, and wondered where the water came from; looked down at old Neptune, at the Tritons piping their wreathed horns, at the heaps of broken rock, the hundred jets that dashed over all.

"O child of the woods," he mournfully said, "the Indian is sorry for thee."

"Why should you be sorry?" asked the sculptor.

"Listen! It sighs! Come with Garangula. He will lead thee back to the woods and rocks and thou wilt sing there all the days, with no sadness in thy music — glad to be with thy mother."

"We must lose something for everything we gain," said the sculptor. "It is the law. Millions of people have rhapsodized over this fountain here, whereas it would have been known only to birds and beasts had it stayed at home."

Garangula made no answer.

As they left the fountain, the shadow of Mazaro fell across the waters.

The next day, when working hours were over, the artist took Garangula to the sculpture gallery at the Capitol. They walked down the long hall looking at the statues on either side, Garangula lingering in front of a small bust of Cleopatra, which impressed him as bearing a close resemblance to Zulona. It was almost like seeing her; he would leave it, look back, then return. But nothing moved him deeply till he reached the room containing the Dying Gladiator. As he stood before this, he trembled, his breast heaved; there were tears in his eyes when he raised his head and looked toward the door at the Faun of Praxitiles—the effect was magical— soon he was standing in front of it, making a low, *staccato* sound that did not surprise the sculptor as much as it would have Lord Carleton, who had never known him to laugh.

Then he turned to the figure of a little child on

the right of the faun. It had a sweet, innocent expression, and held a dove to its bosom. A snake was winding around the head of the child. The Indian looked long and earnestly at the symbol of the "Human Soul," then glided swiftly down the stairway, leaving the bewildered sculptor alone.

Following, he found him standing on the hill, *Piazza Campidoglio* His eyes looked beyond the Castle of St. Angelo, St. Peter's, the Tiber winding its way among the thousand memories of the past. The Indian saw them not—he was among the hills, in the clouds, and his face grew peaceful again.

Life in Rome seems so unreal, the most commonplace dreamer finds himself caught up in the heavens, going away, he knows not whither, or cares; he loses all identity with this life. It would be easier to live, love, and die in Rome than elsewhere.

The sculptor and Garangula slowly walked from the Coliseum, under the Arch of Titus, the design of which was curiously examined by the Indian. They might have been in a desert—so alone they were, so isolated the ruins—a few broken columns, a heap of stone—the monuments of a glory forever past, and so unrelated to Now, that when a military band played a national air on the Campagna, the Indian shivered, and said: "The music is strange."

From the Palace of the Cæsars they strolled idly along to the Forum, where they sat down on the broad stone steps. The music of the band grew fainter, till all was silence in the ruins. Finally, the sculptor tired of dreaming, touched his companion.

Garangula looked at him, and said: "The Indian is not here."

CHAPTER FORTY-EIGHTH.

"Angels and ministers of grace defend us."
Shakespeare

GARANGULA showed no interest as they walked through the Borghese Gallery, filled with statues, life-size, and portrait busts—all from hands that the world holds sacred. The sculptor stopped before Canova's Venus, hoping that would arouse him—the Indian looked at the reclining figure, but said nothing. The sculptor thought, "After all, perhaps I am mistaken in his appreciation."

The Indian felt the thought, and hastened to remedy any seeming rudeness.

"Nay, do not be disappointed in Garangula, the Indian; he is only a child of nature. The influences in the forest," and he looked at the grounds of the Villa Borghese, "are clinging to him still. Garangula sees nothing in these to-day."

"What influences?" asked the sculptor, trying to conceal his annoyance.

"At first, Garangula felt the joyousness of the woods, then as he walked under the trees, it seemed as if he had been there before, that he belonged to that time, and he was here now in a dream."

The sculptor looked at him with doubt. 'Perhaps Raphael's spirit kept you company," said he, smiling. "He used to walk in the early mornings under those ilex trees."

"Who was Raphael?"

The question and interest were so unfeigned, the sculptor was in a good humor at once—the very novelty interested him.

"Come, we will walk along the paths he used to stroll, while I tell you of the divine artist."

Garangula's face glowed as he listened. They walked down the slope of the hill, crossed a rivulet that ran softly by the old trees, too modest to sing with the fountains. Once, when much moved the Indian knelt and plucked a wildflower from the hillside, and placed it in his bosom. The sculptor talked earnestly. From the *Porta del Popolo* they went to the Pincian Hill, where Garangula examined the marble busts of great men, hoping to find Raphael's. The band was playing on the Pincio, but Garangula heeded it not.

Before leaving London, Lord Carleton took him to the opera several weeks in succession. The Englishman had never been so pleased with his protege; his exquisite delight, his soul speaking through his eyes as he listened, impressed Lord Carleton anew with his poetic nature. Once, in the midst of an opera, the Indian turned to him, and said: "Garangula hears the echoes of the Great Spirit's voice above the music. There!" and he listened with an intensity that was almost a pain, "The voice is with the music!"

But he heard not the band on the Pincio, neither did he hear the sculptor talking as they walked to the foot of the Hill, where they separated for the night—the sculptor going to his chambers, the Indian returning to the studio where he lay on the landing till far into the night, thinking of the divine artist.

The sculptor went with the Indian to all of the galleries in the old palaces—the Kircheriano, the Colonna, the Sciarra, Tirlonia Tabularium, the Corsini, the Vatican, and others. These visits were interspersed with walks on the Campagna and drives beyond Rome. The drives in the country where all things spoke of the past, even more than in Rome, impressed the Indian as did the Borghese grounds—he felt related to the ruins; peculiarly was this true of the Appian Way.

As he looked up at the sky, the clouds the angels came down to paint—the tombs by the wayside, he seemed to remember something that grew more and more mysterious.

This sight-seeing had occupied nearly nine months, the sculptor reserving the Vatican for the last, and when the time came, he was eager to go to that wonderful palace of art.

Passing by the *Portone di Bronze* by the right

colonnade of the *Piazza* of St. Peter, the Swiss guard conducted them to the *Maggiordomato* to receive their *permesso*. The Indian was much interested in the costume of the guard; each looked at the other's dress, and with evident admiration. Garangula's dress drew but slight attention in Rome, where congregate so many nationalities. Many supposed he belonged to the Forestieri, dressed in a picturesque garb to attract artists.

They went up to the *Scala Regia*, the long flight of stairs unheeded by the Indian, who studied the tunnel vaulting overhead as he walked lightly, then turned to a side entrance that led to the Sistine Chapel. The sculptor was little rewarded here. Michael Angelo's frescoes on the ceiling that have been famed for more than three centuries, had no meaning to the Indian. He could in no wise comprehend God Almighty in the air, separating light from darkness; neither could he understand the Demon and the various characters between the Creation and the Last Judgment. To this Indian, there had never been any darkness or devil. He looked at first with some interest, but the confusion of it all grew more and more hopeless.

It was pleasant to observe that when the Indian could not comprehend a thing, he did not criticise it, or feel disturbed that he saw no beauty.

As the Indian left the Chapel, the sculptor smiled, remembering his own boyhood days in the old home, where he was taught to adore Michael Angelo, and led to believe there could not by any possibility, ever be another so gifted. He had worshiped him during all the years from the time he named his pet dogs for the old master, till he dreamed of living in the same land that gave him birth; when he would receive his highest inspiration standing in this chapel. The sculptor had passed through the many stages others have done, had his altars torn down, leaving but a cold, dead feeling that no enthusiasm in after years can revive—so one thinks at the time, till he takes heart to look at the best this great man has done, studies his life, the history of the times in which he lived, all he had to contend with—then the painter, sculptor, poet, is given a place not so high, perhaps, still above many others.

They were before Raphael's Transfiguration— Garangula looked at the One face in the picture with an expression the sculptor could not wholly understand, but when his eyes wandered from this to the others, the look changed to disgust and horror—he turned quickly away. The sculptor was at first astonished, then his face broke into a smile followed by a laugh which the Indian did not hear.

When they entered *Raphael's Stanze*, the bearing of the Indian changed.

Long after, his companion recalled with delight Garangula's appreciation in the Vatican, also when they went to see the picture of "Sacred and Profane Love."

The sculptor led the way to Titian's picture, and told the Indian its title, then asked with much curiosity—"Which do you think is the Sacred Love?"

"Garangula knows not what thou dost mean by 'profane love', but this one belongs to the Happy Hunting-Grounds, and is here on a sojourn to let us know what beautiful love is there," he said, looking at the figure representing Sacred Love.

Titian stole the colors of heaven for this picture, and the brush was dipped in the Celestial Fire, to paint the nude figure of Sacred Love. If, by chance, one glance from this to the nude figures by other artists, he turns and leaves the room, lest the impression of "Sacred and Profane Love" be effaced by hideous realism in form and color. Reaching the door, he looks back at Titian's picture, with a half-uttered prayer that its memory will go with him through life, throwing a halo of sanctity over all his thoughts.

"Sacred Love" though nude, is clothed in Immortality. "Profane Love" is draped, but buffalo robes would not hide its nakedness.

CHAPTER FORTY-NINTH.

"As fragrant incense on the air,
So mount to heaven my early prayer;
And let my hands uplifted be,
As evening sacrifice to thee."
Psalms.

IT was in the sculpture gallery of the Vatican. They glanced hastily at the collection of antiquities, passing to the room containing sculpture, on to the *Cortile del Belvedere*. The Indian smiled sympathetically at the Molossian Hounds that mark the entrance to this octagonal court, and stopped before the famous group of the Laocoön—but his face bore a look of pain that did not vanish till he reached the second corner of the cabinet, where a wonderful transformation took place.

The sculptor remained behind looking at

some dancing figures. It was not a free day in the Vatican, besides, it was a gloomy one for that place, and there was no one near when the Indian entered the cabinet of Apollo Belvedere.

Motionless he gazed at that superb work of art, of which Winckelmann says: "At the aspect of the Belvedere Apollo, I forget all the universe. I involuntarily assume the most noble attributes of my being in order to be worthy of its presence." The Indian took off his turban, raised his head loftily, folded his arms high on his breast. Then he walked to the side of the pedestal and took the attitude of Apollo. He was poised, ready to step forward with all the agility that belongs to the native Indian, his arm in the attitude of holding the ægis; he looked the god.

Standing there, looking up at Apollo, the divine expressed itself. Flinging aside his robe, he stepped in front of the statue and improvised in such rapid succession, the sculptor, who had approached unseen, was bewildered at the transition he made from one pose to ano'her, the meaning of which was felt rather than understood.

The sculptor thought: "Is he mad? I have at times almost believed he might be."

But as he watched the perfect representation, he smiled with chagrin, and said: "My model is a great man in disguise. How amused he must have been at my patronizing air over his supposed ignorance! I remember many things he said that I would not then understand, but his simplicity soon banished this; and it is the memory of that simplicity which puzzles me now. I thought the gods had returned to earth when first I saw him—I know it now! I am transported to the shades of Olympus and behold the gods."

The Indian's motion changed. He related and connected scenes from the Greek tragedies, at least, so they appeared to the sculptor.

"Ye gods!" he cried. "What conception! What dignity! What grandeur! What poetry! For the first time I know the full meaning of that quotation—'Tragedy, majestic tragedy, is worthy to stand before the sanctuary of Truth, and to be held priestess of her oracles.' A flood of light illuminates all art!"

The sculptor's dreaming was forgotten. Art became a living, breathing Truth to him, and this feeling created a resolution that set his whole being afire.

The Indian was lost in the poet, and a divinity enveloped him. These improvisations glided on imperceptibly at first, into something the sculptor could not describe, save they brought thoughts of "Sacred Love."

"Above Garangula's head," the sculptor afterward said, "I saw that figure float and look down upon him. Garangula's face shone with a light not of this world. He seemed looking into the 'Happy Hunting-Grounds'. 'Transfiguration!' I exclaimed. What influenced me I knew not, neither do I know what next transpired—the one thing I remember is, that after a time I raised my head and found myself kneeling alone. I arose and walked humbly down the flight of steps, passed the Vatican Gardens, and reached St. Peter's Square, where I found the sun shining through the clouds, and saw Garangula standing near the great obelisk, looking at the rainbow on the fountain."

CHAPTER FIFTIETH.

"......And then, what's brave, what's noble,
Let's do it after the high Roman fashion,"
Shakespeare.

THE next day there was an air of work in the studio; sketches hastily done were scattered on the table, bits of clay lay on the floor, a plaster cast, an unfinished bust or two, and a block of marble on the landing.

This continued for many weeks, the sculptor rarely taking rest till evening. Garangula watched his work, asking many questions; he was deeply interested in the bronze statue of Homer — the different processes which it had undergone, from the first rough sketch to the embodiment it now was. The sculptor took pleasure in explaining to him the details, often illustrating from the object.

He worked on, never satisfied—he had seen Garangula in the attitudes at the Vatican. The Indian remembered them vaguely. Had the sculptor been an artist in its broadest sense—having an understanding of the divine, the Indian would have given him yet higher expression than that in the Vatican, for Garangula wrought from the soul.

One day after continued effort, the sculptor said, "I am very tired, Garangula—let us rest; I am discouraged as well," and the two left the studio together.

They went to the grounds of the Colonna Palace, and found themselves alone. The quiet walks, bordered with flowers, the birds singing, the peaceful company of the Indian, soon restored the sculptor's habitual frame of mind.

"Let us go into the gallery," at length he said; "I wish you to see a portrait of Vittoria Colonna, and when we return, I will tell you a story."

The dear little face of Vittoria, taken when three or four years old, peeps out from a quaint cap and rich old-fashioned dress; the child-like simplicity is so true, one expects it to step from the frame and put up its rosy lips to be kissed. This was so real to the Indian that he looked back, and said: "Garangula loves the little princess."

"It is easy to divine the beautiful woman, so loved by the great master," replied the sculptor.

Then he told the Indian the love-dream of Michael Angelo. The Indian listened reverently—an expression at once humble and holy, came over his face. And when the sculptor repeated the lines Angelo wrote to Vittoria Colonna, the Indian bowed his head, and answered: "O Love, thou art very beautiful!"

When they arose to return, he said: "Speak again the words of the great master."

His companion gave the lines: "As a stone, when an intaglio is cut upon it, becomes more precious than in its natural state, so am I of greater worth since your image has been graven on my heart. When a sculptor would give shape to an idea, he makes a mould in some base material, such as clay or wax; then he puts it into marble and secures its immortality, so I, born but the model of my future self, have been re-formed and re-made by you, O lofty and noble lady, in more perfect expression."

These were the last words he spoke to the Indian.

They had now reached the gates. From some unaccountable impulse, the sculptor clasped the Indian's hand, and they separated for the night.

CHAPTER FIFTY-FIRST.

> "That so the race which was to come
> These things might learn and know;
> And sons unborn, who should arise,
> Might to their sons them show."
>
> Psalm 78=6

THE next morning, the Indian disrobed himself as usual, and waited in the studio. But the sculptor came not.

In searching for a sketch that had interested him the day before, Garangula drew aside a curtain that concealed a large mirror extending to the floor.

After a few moments, he said softly: "Garangula, the Indian, is beautiful."

And as he looked, his love of beauty, the knowledge unfolded through Zulona, and who shall say from what far-away past? — swept nearer and nearer the surface, until, as by a miracle, they burst in all their power, enveloping him! He closed his eyes and said: "The Great Spirit is touching Garangula, the Indian!"

At last, he opened his eyes, took up a chisel, and said: "Garangula will make a statue."

He looked in the mirror and began to copy himself. Then another thought came—"Garangula will make a statue of his forefather bidding farewell to Tehuacana Hills. It shall be a memorial unto his mother's people. Their lives were beautiful. Yes, Garangula will leave a memorial unto them."

He clothed himself in skins, dressed as an Indian Chieftain, and worked on. When night came he was still alone in the studio. The sculptor returned not for a long while. Garangula thought of him many times, but was completely absorbed in his work.

One day a man laboriously climbed the outer wall of the Diocletian baths — he reached the window of the studio, and looked. He turned deathly pale, and cried: "Ye powers, help me!

Garangula is growing further and further from me. Stay his hand—dull his brain"— A cloud of smoke gathered about Mazaro's head; it grew darker—his hold relaxed, he fell to the ground, crying: "The circle of Rome is around Garangula."

The Indian left the piece of marble on which he began, and modeled his statues in clay; taking them through the final stage of progression, becoming the bronze figures seen at the exhibition.

And while he wrought, he said: "As a stone when an intaglio is cut upon it, becomes more precious than in its natural state, so am I of greater worth since your image has been graven on my heart." As he repeated the last lines, "have been re-formed and re-made by you, O lofty and noble lady, in more perfect expression," a mysterious force filled the room, and as it increased, Garangula gained in power of execution.

* * * * * * *

The time had come. Garangula looked at the

statues for the last time. He was deeply moved, but spake no word.

Taking a cloth, he slowly draped them, and walked to the doorway, then turned and gave a look of love. Behold! Above the bronze figures, the Mysterious Force had centered. It filled his being with power.

His spirit inquired, "What is this?"

Then there appeared a beauteous form.

"It is GENIUS," was the answer. "And it will be with you Forever."

And the beauteous form vanished.

Then, like the grand Chieftain he had portrayed, the Indian went forth unheralded and unknown.

CHAPTER FIFTY-SECOND.

> "I am a brother to dragons and a companion to owls."
>
> Job 30. 29.

SOON after the Indian left the studio, the sculptor, pale and emaciated, feebly climbed the flight of steps. He had been so ill he had thought little about Garangula, but supposed, without any reasoning, that he would be there.

He was therefore disappointed to find the rooms empty. No, not empty—there were two draped figures! He approached them slowly. Curiously, and with a feeling of awe, he lifted the drapery. The Indian Chief, standing on the brow of a hill, looked far away—beyond—into the land of which he had been dispossessed. He stood, proud, fearless, and alone, his head thrown haughtily back; his powerful figure seemed poised in air, it was so far above the ignominy that had been heaped upon him.

It was a memorial indeed! Greater than any poets have sung—a reminder that the red man who roamed the forests, was nearer a god than men deemed.

When the sculptor caught sight of this statue so well wrought, he trembled, and cried: "Who hath done this? This is immortality, and it is not mine! Someone has stolen into my studio and done this work—someone has robbed me of my model!"

Excitedly, he went to the other figure and raised the veil. It was the same form, slightly bent; the proud head was now bowed, and the whole figure told the sad story that he was looking on Tehuacana Hills for the last time, and was going forth, alone forever.

A hero conquered! But it was the "Victory of the vanquished."

The sculptor rose, bewildered and faint, then became so blind and dizzy that he groped for something to support himself; but this time it was not physical weakness alone—Temptation entered the studio that had known such purity and peace

Why not give these statues to the world as his? The tempter said. Were they not in his studio? And who had a right to go there and work? Besides, who would know? Could he not bring in the critics, invite many to come and see, and would not all declare they had seen them there, and if he who made them, came, could he not easily prove him an impostor? Even the founders could not testify against him—he would say the man who went to them, was employed by himself. And so the tempter continued.

The sculptor's agitation increased. He walked nervously up and down the room. At last, the fame so long desired, should be his! His dreaming had not been realized, but the world would think so.

He threw himself on the ground exhausted, and said: "I will wait here till morning, and then—well, then perhaps I will call the people."

Twilight stole in—the two bronze figures stood

solemn and grand and lonely in the semi-darkness. Beside them lay the young artist, and singularly enough, he had thrown himself almost under the raised foot of the Indian.

A story was told in that studio in Rome while the darkness gathered in. Did the good angel come and bend over the tempted one while he slept his troubled sleep?

When the first rays of light crept through the window and fell on the bronze figures, the sculptor looked around with bewildered air—arose, and remembered all.

He looked at the figures till the light grew stronger and fell full upon them—then he cried out: "No, I cannot do it! I shrink from an act so cowardly and ignoble. These grand old Chieftains inspire me with a power I have not known. I, too, will carve that which men will look upon. O my goddess, thou hast a new charm for me! I have a holy feeling for thee now! This is Art! This is Truth! I will call the people and tell them the truth."

That morning the strange story was told, and the excitement began. Who was the artist? If he would only come forth, he should be crowned with the laurel, as in days of old.

When Lord Carleton heard all, he at once exclaimed: "Garangula has done this work! I believed it when I first saw them at the Exhibition — I have always known he was great; I must see him once more!"

Lord Carleton sought long. Rome waited.

THE END.

www.ingramcontent.com/pod-product-compliance
Lightning Source LLC
Chambersburg PA
CBHW022104230426
43672CB00008B/1279